WILDWOOD

top left: **This photograph studio shot from the early 1900s shows Charles Kelpe as the driver, with William Kesselring on the right.**

top right: **St. Onge pioneer family.**

above: **St. Paul Vacation Bible School.**

right: **The Krueger and Kajewicz families, along with friends and related families, met on Sundays to rest and socialize. In the center of the photo is the family's patriarch, Martin Krueger. He was the German immigrant ancestor for many area families.**

top: Raccoon trappers.

middle: left, **Fick children**; right, **Dreinhofer ladies in Pond**.

bottom: left, **Wildwood residents at an early Wildwood Day celebration. Longtime city councilman Ron James is pictured in front on the left. Ron Marcantano, who later became mayor, is pictured on the right.**

WILDWOOD

BY JO BECK

Copyright © 2009, Reedy Press, LLC.
All rights reserved.

Reedy Press
PO Box 5131,
St. Louis, MO 63139, USA

No part of this publication may be reproduced or transmitted in any form or by any means, electronic or mechanical, including photocopy, recording, or any information storage and retrieval system, without permission in writing from the publisher.

Permissions may be sought directly from Reedy Press at the above mailing address or via our website at www.reedypress.com.

Library of Congress Control Number: 2009920365

ISBN: 978-1-933370-80-4

Please visit our website at www.reedypress.com.

Printed in the United States of America
09 10 11 12 13   5 4 3 2 1

CONTENTS

Preface   ix

Introduction   1

Chapter 1: The City of Wildwood   33

Chapter 2: Recreation   43

Chapter 3: Community Organizations   67

Chapter 4: Schools   85

Chapter 5: Churches   95

Bibliography   100

DEDICATION

I owe many thanks to Dovie Poertner Berry, pictured here, and her wonderful cousins, Dorothy Krueger Pendleton, Bebe Poertner McKenzie, and Irene Gaehle Hairston (1918–2007). They are all keepers of history. Dovie, in particular, has been prolific throughout her life with research on local history and genealogical topics, and she is a gifted storyteller. These ladies have always joked that they are like the land turtles that are so common here. They've never strayed far from where they grew up in the Wildwood area; as a consequence, they know everything and everyone from our area's past. Along with dozens of other local residents too numerous to list here, they have saved hundreds of photos and artifacts, and they remember events and personalities that make our history come to life. I feel blessed to look into the past through their eyes.

PREFACE

A chance meeting with two residents gave me a rare look into Wildwood's past and piqued my interest in learning more about the hills and valleys, the charming country lanes named for early settlers, and the remnants of earlier settlements. In 1996, on a visit to Rockwoods Reservation, I met two older women who had lived there as children in the 1920s and 1930s.

Their Cherokee grandmother had instructed the women in the use of native plants as medicinal herbs, and they were happy to show these to me, telling how they were used to cure headaches, fever, and other ailments. Just a short walk off the roadway and the hiking paths, we found many wildflowers and plants that they named as medicinal.

At the clear running spring, we picked a sprig of watercress and tasted the spicy, radishy flavor of the plant. I had thought I knew the park and its features well, from long hikes and bike rides along the many trails, but I had never noticed the cress growing there before. They told how their grandmother and mother used the watercress not only for remedies, but in salads, sandwiches, and other dishes.

"The spring was bigger then," they said, and they pointed at the hills all around the Glencoe valley where we stood. "There were many springs besides this one, but most of them have dried up now," they added.

Now as I approach the spring in any season, I have a different, much richer viewpoint of this natural area. It is no longer a paved roadside leading to the visitor center, but a dusty dirt road through a community that once thrived here before the suburban houses.

Surely, old Ninian Hamilton, who built a grist mill less than half a mile away on his Spanish land grant, must have come to this same spring. Indians, trappers, and traders stopped at the spring and camped nearby, along the banks of the stream that we now call Hamilton-Carr Creek. Indian dwellings stood nearby; the Meramec River was their highway. A big oaken bucket hung at the spring for all to use, and children were sent there every day to fetch water. The miner's railway rumbled, carrying lumber and stone to St. Louis. Dynamite boomed. Workers shouted at the mules pulling the loads of clay, and the limestone kilns crackled twenty-four hours a day. The telltale smoke from the moonshiner's copper coils hung in the treetops, and the steam from caves breathed into the air on cold winter mornings.

The industry is gone now, but the rocks, hills, and plants remain. I remember the stories of the oldsters, tales of events, people, and places.

Funny, now that I know their names, I see these plants everywhere. So it is with history. The more we know of it, the more valuable it becomes to us. The aim of this book is to give readers a glimpse into this valuable history and the many resources in Wildwood, one of Missouri's newest cities.

The spring at Rockwood is just one of many natural wonders in our area. As I travel along the stream, at first I see only a quick glance of the bright green leaves, clinging tenuously to the soil at the creek side or in the bottom of the rocky stream. The closer I get to the spring, I see more and more clumps of the cress. The watercress grows only in clear running water and can be seen around the spring even in winter snow. At the rock's opening, where the water continually flows from the hillside, the plant grows abundantly, blooming with a modest white flower in summer. It never fails to make me smile and remember the wonderful stories that opened my eyes to the beauty and history of this place.

INTRODUCTION

Wildwood is in a class by itself when it comes to quality of life. Long-range planning, an emphasis on family living, and lots of community amenities all add up to a first-class community. Based on these factors, *Money Magazine* named Wildwood as one of the "Best Places to Live in America" in 2003.

Blue-ribbon Rockwood schools, a new St. Louis Community College campus, a growing town center, comprehensive fire and police services, updated roads and infrastructure, our own YMCA branch, and recreational opportunities such as parks and trails are all big factors in the quality of life.

The City of Wildwood has played a leading role in this investment in the future with improvements such as parks, roadways, bridges, trails, and landscaping. The city values preservation of historic structures. In addition, it has forged partnerships with other area organizations to bring quality services and amenities to residents.

From the city's beginnings, the Parks and Recreation Department has been proactive in sponsoring community celebrations and events such as the Wildwood Celebration, trail hikes, walk/run events, movie nights in the new town center, city concerts, and classes for residents.

* * *

INTRODUCTION

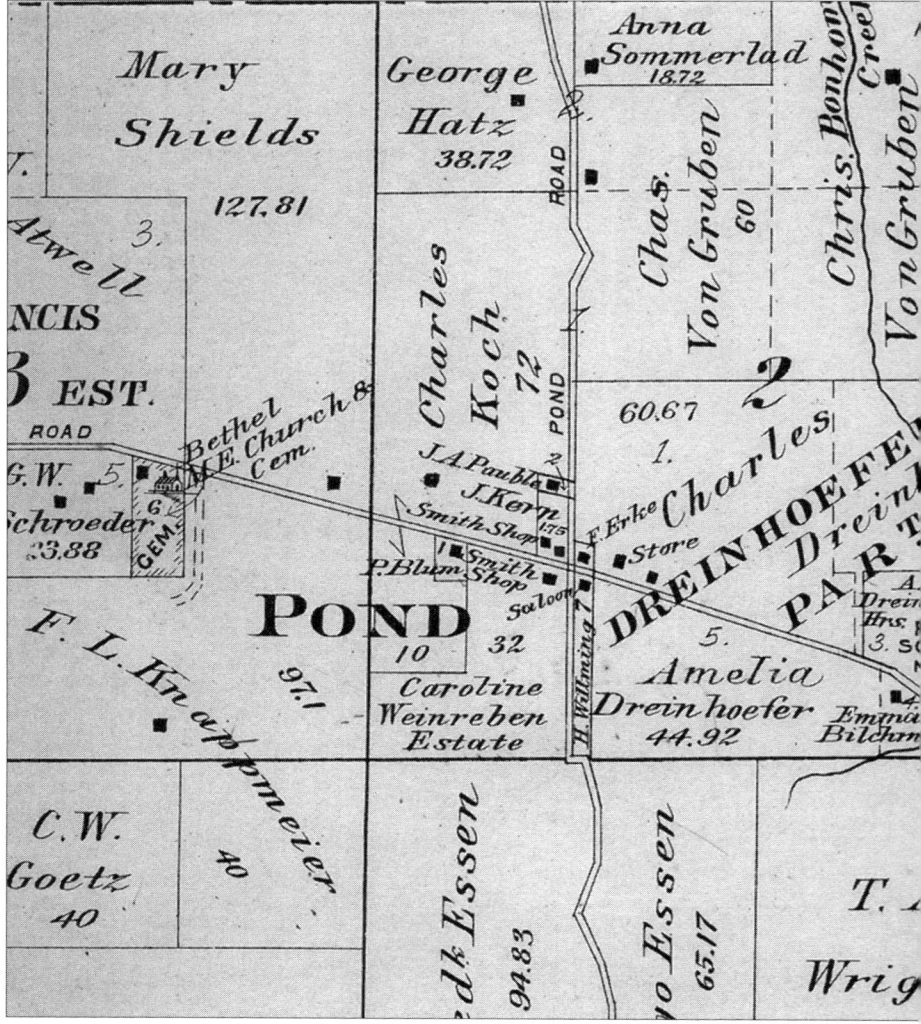

As Missouri achieved statehood in 1821, the old maps were redrawn and the Wildwood area became part of Meramec Township in St. Louis County. These old Meramec Township maps that follow show how the Wildwood area looked in 1909.

Note that Manchester Road is pictured running through the center of this 1909 Plat book map of St. Louis County's Meramec Township. It shows the area between Pond and Grover. Although both villages were absorbed by the City of Wildwood, local residents sometimes refer to the old town names. The jewel of this area is the beautifully restored Old Pond School, just east of the newer elementary school that bears the same name. Just west of Pond Elementary is a new brick building that houses Wildwood Middle School. Bethel Church is at the far left of the map. Prominent landowners noted on the map included Dreinhofer, Von Gruben, Wright, Hatz, Koch, Essen, and Knappmeier. Construction of a state highway passing through

INTRODUCTION

Wildwood in 1835 connected St. Louis to Jefferson City. In 1851, an extension of the railroad into the area made a huge impact on these tiny frontier outposts, reconnecting them to St. Louis. Over time, simple stagecoach stops and train depots evolved into business districts, many complete with post office, school, blacksmith shop, stores, and the ever-popular tavern.

Landowners named on this map included Hiller, Brown, Kern, Deutschmann, Eatherton, Wulf, and Hoehne. Grover was originally named St. Friedling. During the term of President Grover Cleveland, the postmaster, loyal Democrat John Brown, renamed the post office in honor of the popular president. Presumably, local Republicans didn't raise a fuss, and so the name stuck. Today, the village of Grover is included in the Town Center area of Wildwood.

INTRODUCTION

A depiction of the earliest settlers in the region.

Early History

A brief history of our area will show the forces that shaped our modern city. The first Americans to settle in Wildwood migrated here along the region's waterways more than ten thousand years ago. Remnants of settlements and artifacts found along Fox Creek and elsewhere in Wildwood shows that many Native Americans were living here.

Daniel Boone moved to Missouri in 1798, luring many settlers to follow him. Like Boone, many of the earliest settlers were originally from the Eastern seaboard, with stops along the way in Kentucky and Tennessee. At the time the white settlers came, the land was

INTRODUCTION

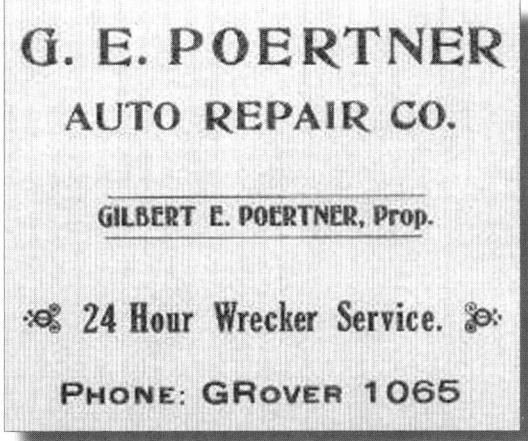

"This advertisement is from my father's business," said Bebe Poertner McKenzie, a Wildwood resident. "He traveled all over the Wildwood area and did a good business with the towing. It was ten dollars for a tow. One place he had to go every week was to that big Monarch Hill, heading down into the valley from Wild Horse Creek. Every Saturday night someone would hit the telephone pole along those hairpin curves and they'd call to have him pull them out of the ditch. Dad always said 'that's my ten-dollar telephone pole!'"

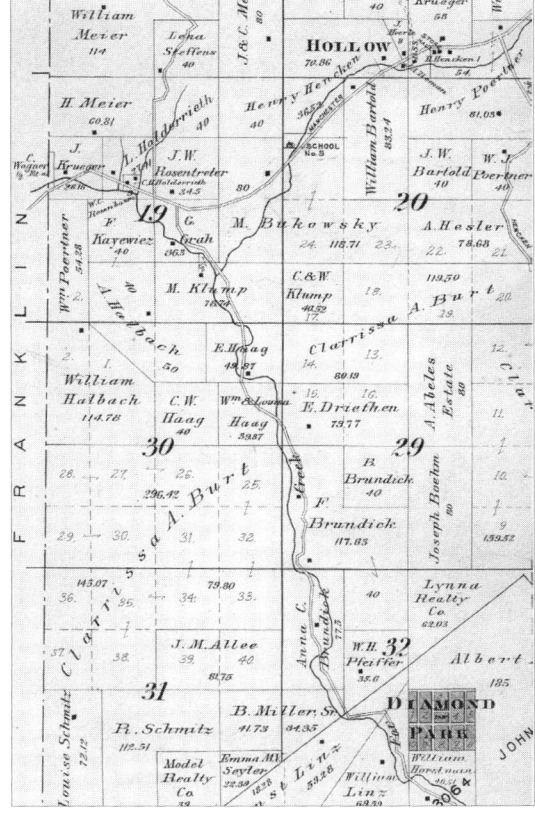

The village of Hollow, located on Highway 100 in far west Wildwood, about five miles west of Highway 109, is shown in the upper right corner of this 1909 Meramec Township map. This village's name started as "Deutsch Hollow," so called by the German settlers. "They liked the way this valley—or hollow—looked like their homeland," said Hollow historian, Bebe McKenzie. Later, the name was shortened to Hollow. Not much remains of the old settlement except a few houses and the historic dance hall and roadhouse called Stovall's Grove. This hamlet was once a busy stagecoach stop, and in the mid-1900s when the road carried more traffic, there were a number of stores and other businesses in the area. Manchester Road travels west from Hollow to the Franklin County line, which forms Wildwood's western border. Fox Creek Road, running parallel to the meandering Fox Creek, travels down the middle of the map. It is undoubtedly one of Wildwood's most picturesque roadways.

South of Wildwood, Fox Creek empties into the Meramec River. Fox Creek has been named one of St. Louis County's most pristine waterways. On several occasions residents and activists have fought real estate developers to maintain the stream quality. At the bottom of the map are three parcels of land once owned by real estate developers. One platted out a subdivision called "Diamond Park." A current-day road leading up "Fox Creek Mountain" in south Wildwood bears the name of Model Realty, another turn-of-the-century developer. Horse farms and heavily wooded areas are commonplace here. Like most areas in Wildwood, the population density here is low. Most homeowners have lots of three acres or more. Prominent landowners listed in this map section included Halbach, Klump, Bukowsky, Grauer, Meier, Krueger, Poertner, Bartold, Haag, Burt, and Brundick.

INTRODUCTION

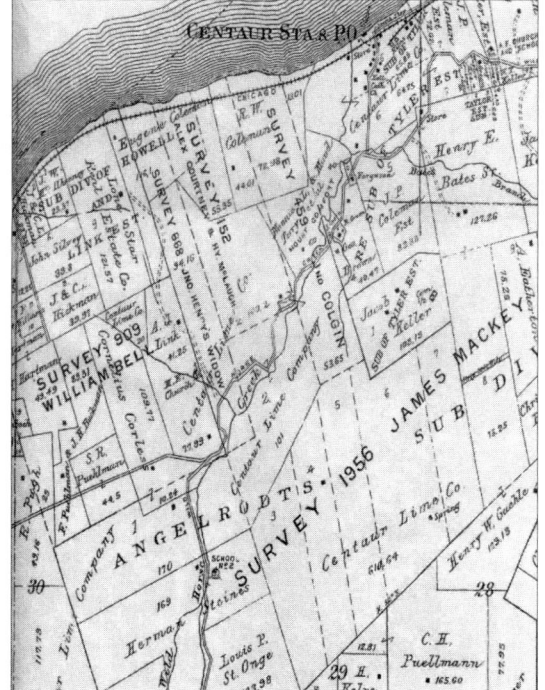

This old map shows the northwest corner of what is now Wildwood. Some of Wildwood's most exclusive housing is found here, and horse farms are common. The Missouri River is at the top of the map, and landowners named include the Tyler and Coleman families, both early settlers. The Chicago, Rock Island, and Pacific Railroad ran through this area. An important road, then and now, was Wild Horse Creek Road, which meanders through the center of this map, looping around the western and northern border of the 2,441-acre Babler State Park, which is noted for its forested, rugged terrain. The company town of Centaur is shown on the south bank of the river, and a large land tract is labeled with the Centaur Lime Company. Anton Leiweke owned this company. Other landowners noted were Puellman, Bates, Howell, Mackey, Kelpe, St. Onge, Keller, Corless, Gaehle, and Steines.

still a vast wilderness governed by the Spanish. Only game paths and trappers' trails penetrated the dense forest. Ninian Hamilton received a Spanish land grant in the Glencoe area in 1803. Some of his original land became Rockwoods Reservation (ca. 1938), and some of it became La Salle Institute (ca. 1872).

After the territory became part of the United States, early pioneers established a trading post near today's La Salle Springs Middle School to accommodate the increasing number of adventurers who began pouring into the area intent on exploring and exploiting its abundant natural resources. The first post office in Wildwood (ca. 1827) was at the corner of Bouquet Road and Old Manchester Road near the Franklin County Line.

INTRODUCTION

The Missouri River that runs along Wildwood's northern border was full of steamboats in the mid-1800s, especially in the 1850s, the decade before the Civil War. This 1858 newspaper ad shows that there was a regular schedule of steamboats that ran from St. Louis to St. Joseph. One of the steamboat captains was Captain Ben Hutchison, an early settler in Ellisville. There were steamboat docks at St. Albans, Centaur, and other locations, but the main stop in this area was Port Royal, just over the Franklin County line. This dock, adjacent to the railroad tracks, made it a logical shipping point for goods going either east or west. In July of 1835, Frederick Steines wrote, "The rapid development of the State of Missouri is attested to by the rapidly increasing, lively steamboat traffic on the Missouri River. Almost daily steamboats are seen on the river . . . traffic is interrupted each winter for several weeks, and sometimes even for months, by the ice or the flow of ice." Many older residents recalled hearing about the steamboats from their elders. In the first half of the 1900s you could buy a ticket for an evening of music on the water. The pleasure boats departed from Port Royal and came back a few hours later.

Steamboats are specially designed to float in shallow water like the Missouri. Their hulls were only a few feet below the water line, so they were often capsized by tree stumps floating in the water. The boilers often overheated and burst into flames; the all-wood construction of the vessels caused them to burn like tinder.

Riverboat records show that at least one boat was lost in the Port Royal area. *The Emigrant* was a wooden-hulled side-wheel steamboat that burned and was lost on November 19, 1860. The 343-ton boat had only been launched four years before.

James Eatherton came from Virginia and settled in Missouri in the 1820s or 1830s. He married Martha Ball, daughter of Ballwin founder John Ball. Scotsman Peter Kincaid settled on the Missouri River in 1818, later moving to Franklin County where he founded the town of St. Albans. Samuel Stuart came to the Valley Road area in 1832, building a log cabin that still stands today.

This picturesque farmstead, once called "Overbrook Farm" by its owners, the Steines family, is located at 1333 Pond Road. "Squire" Steines was a local justice of the peace. The building contains the original 1796 log cabin constructed by William Hamilton, son of early Wildwood settler Ninian Hamilton.

Steines and Paffrath Families: "Followers of Duden"

Fredrich Steines came to St. Louis in a wave of German immigration prompted by the writings of Gottfried Duden. A German lawyer, Duden had come to the United States in 1824, settling on land near what is now Dutzow. He hired others to farm for him and spent most of his time traveling around the area and writing. He returned to Germany in 1827 and wrote a glowing guidebook called *A Report of a Journey to the Western States of America*, which became hugely popular in Germany.

Later, many people complained that Duden didn't paint a realistic picture of life in pioneer Missouri, but nonetheless, Germans were eager to flee their homeland for a number of political and economic reasons, and the book triggered a flood of German immigration to Missouri. The Steines family, prominent in the Wildwood area, were

INTRODUCTION

among those so called "followers of Duden," as was Charles Paffrath, another early settler. Paffrath, a nephew of the Steines's, settled in the Fox Creek area, owned a tavern on the stage line, and was widely and fondly known as "mine host Dutch (Deutsch) Charlie."

Hermann and Frederich Steines, brothers, are pictured here. So much of what is known about early St. Louis County history has been gleaned from the many letters and diaries of these two industrious and well-educated men. Local farmers dubbed them "Latin farmers" because they knew more about Latin than farming. The Steines letters tell us their impressions of their adopted country, about meeting Native Americans, about customs of the day, and about farming practices. Many descendants of Frederich and Hermann Steines live throughout the St. Louis area today.

Hermann was single; he came first, in 1833. He had been trained as a pharmacist but became a farmer and later served as justice of the peace. Frederich came the following year; he was the leader of a group of Germans from Soligen. He had been a teacher in Germany and taught the first German school in St. Louis. Later, he took up farming. At the time of Frederich and his family's arrival in the

Frederich Steines

Hermann Steines

summer of 1834, there were less than twenty German families in St. Louis. This is his impression of the town: "St. Louis at that time was a very insignificant place with poor and extremely dirty streets . . . at the intersection of Market and Seventh Street was Chouteau's Pond . . . the whole town presented a sad and unattractive appearance. In and along the streets dead horses, sows and swine were occasionally seen and they stayed there for days, thus polluting the air. Under such filthy conditions it is no wonder that the cholera broke out and caused so many deaths . . . such was the city of St. Louis in 1834."

Within days of Frederich Steines's arrival, cholera struck the family, and his wife and children died. Steines later moved to the Tavern Creek area along the Missouri River, remarried, and had a large family.

In the Steines diaries and letters, we find many references to his neighbors, including the names of Kincaid, Ball, Bacon, Engels, Halbach, Gross, Tippet, Lowe, Farnur, Hancock, McKinnon, Kochs, Wirth, Gaw, Zumwalt, and Ridenhour. "(John) Ball and (Peter) Kincaid are planning to plot sites for two towns," Hermann Steines wrote in February of 1834. These plans later became the towns of St. Albans and Ballwin.

Their travels took them all over Franklin and St. Louis Counties. In May of 1834, Hermann wrote, "Today we left Washington and went to DuBois Creek, to Point Labadie and thence to Tavern Creek and Wild Horse Creek. The nearer we came to St. Louis the wilder and more inhospitable did we find the country to be." A few days later, he passed through Chesterfield, which he concluded was "an insignificant place." In 1837, Frederich Steines wrote, "The state road from here to Jefferson City has been surveyed. . . . We shall profit by this road." He noted that the road was scheduled to go by "Captain Ferris's farm." Harvey Ferris was an early Ellisville settler.

INTRODUCTION

Threshing grain with a steam engine on the Steines Farm, Pond Road. This photo was taken by Carrie Von Gruben (Essen). While today's modern combining machines are mobile, these old threshing machines were stationary. Grain such as oats or wheat would be cut by hand and fed into the machine. Huge crews of men were required to keep the threshing operation running smoothly, so the machine would be moved from one farm to another and the farmers would help each other with the harvest.

While the men were harvesting, the women of the neighborhood were slaving away over hot stoves, producing the huge dinner that the workers would expect at the noon meal. Tables would be moved out to the yard, and every sort of delicacy was set before the exhausted men. Then as now, homemade pies were especially prized. "The women cooked everything you could raise on a farm: ham and beef, homemade bread, fresh vegetables, maybe fresh and blackberries or raspberry custard," recalled Don Jaeger. "There would be six different kinds of pie, four or five cakes, coffee and lemonade. One guy I remember always ate a whole pie by himself—and that was after he'd eaten a complete meal all of all that great food. He did that for years. When it came time for pie, he'd always say 'don't bother to cut mine.'" He intended to eat the whole thing by himself and he did.

Frederick W. Steines, a son of Hermann, married Johanna Von Gruben in 1869 and bought a farm just north of Pond. He was a prominent citizen, having served in the Civil War. He served as a school director and a justice of the peace for many years. Another branch of the Steines family lived along Wild Horse Creek Road.

INTRODUCTION

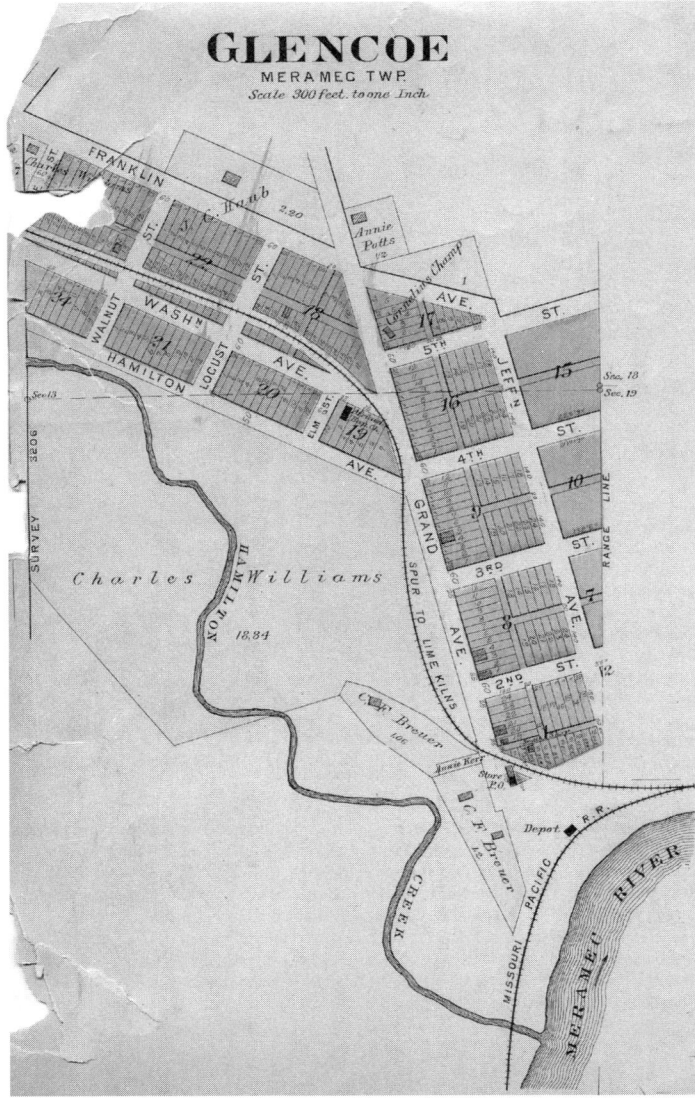

This vintage Glencoe map shows what a booming town it was at the turn of the century. Prominently located near major highways, the railroad line, and the Meramec River, the town boasted of many houses, schools, stores, a blacksmith shop, small manufacturing concerns, a fine railroad depot, and churches, including an African Baptist Church in section 19. Note the Missouri Pacific Railroad line running alongside the Meramec River. This old rail line is now a multi-use recreational area called the Al Foster Trail and is well used by hikers, walkers, and bikers. Hamilton Creek runs along the southern border of the town, which hugged the valley floor. Meramec River flooding in the 1980s and 1990s devastated much of the town, and it now contains a cluster of homes, a church, and the Wabash model railroad headquarters. Much of the town has been designated as parkland.

INTRODUCTION

A hiking trail in Babler State Park commemorates this early settler and his family. Henry Kelpe, II, was eight years old when he and his parents came to the Centaur area from Germany. After his marriage to Caroline Arbegast, Henry bought a forty-acre farm for $6.25 an acre, and the Kelpe family farmed it until the mid-1930s, when it was sold to make way for the park. In addition to farming, Henry was a blacksmith. He also served as postmaster for the area, which came to be called Kelpe. His descendants remain in the area. Henry died in 1923 at the age of seventy-eight.

Other Early Settlers

Robert Coleman and his family came to our area in 1837. He bought land between the Missouri River and Wild Horse Creek. When Robert died around 1849, his sons William and Robert took over the farm. Both brothers had around four hundred acres, owned African American slaves to work the land, and produced crops such as oats, wheat, corn, and hemp.

INTRODUCTION

This charming old cabin, located at 2261 Valley Road in Wildwood, was built in 1832 by the Stuart family. It is in excellent condition, surrounded by an acre of gardens and the adjoining two-story farmhouse that the Stuart family built in 1912 when they vacated the cabin. Owners Ray and Mary Joseph have lovingly maintained both structures, and they have preserved the history and some artifacts from the Stuart family.

The Tyler family also arrived in 1837 and settled near the Colemans. Around 1840, the Tyler family owned over one thousand acres. They also had slaves, and they raised pigs and sheep and grew grain crops. In Babler Park, there are cemeteries where the Tylers and the Colemans are buried, but the resting places of their slaves are not there, or at least not in marked graves. Other families buried in Babler Park include the surnames of Bates, Kroenung, Puellman, Glaser, and Bothe.

Former slaves also became landowners here. In the Church Road area, William West bought land after he earned his freedom from Lawrence Long. West's descendants still live in the Wildwood area today.

INTRODUCTION

top: This remarkable old photo comes from the Kroenung family. Note that the three men seated in front are a horn player, a fiddler, and a harpist. Joseph Kroenung, the harpist, is the only person identified in the photo.

right: "This lady's real name was Mrs. Mershinsky, but around the neighborhood we called her 'Tanta Shinsky,'" recalled Stan Kreienkamp, who grew up on Bouquet Road. She is pictured here holding a newborn baby. "She was a kindly old woman and everyone loved her. She'd come when a baby was born, to help the new mother, or she came when someone was sick." Kreienkamp added. "Tanta" means "aunt" in German. Mary Mershinsky was the mother of Charlie Schlemper, a Fox Creek farmer. Ivan Schlemper, Mrs. Mershinsky's grandson, recalls that his grandmother lived with their family from the time she was widowed until her death. "Any time someone from the area needed help—all the way from Gray Summit to Grover—they'd come and get her to stay with them," said Schlemper. The beloved "Tanta" is buried in the Schlemper family plot of the old Pacific cemetery.

In the ensuing years, farmers, lumbermen, quarrymen, and even real estate entrepreneurs radiating west from the fledgling riverfront town of St. Louis made their way into the region, all inexorably and indelibly modifying the landscape. As the population grew, scattered small villages sprang up, one tied to the other by wagon roads, familial bonds, and everlasting friendships.

INTRODUCTION

This historic home, located just north of Eureka, is one of Wildwood's oldest, and it has a fascinating history. Built on a 250-foot bluff above the river, it has a splendid view of the Meramec River Valley. It is believed that the home was built between 1813 and 1818. When businessman James Broderick bought it in 1895, it was said to be eighty years old. He named it River Craig. Broderick was impressed with the home's four limestone fireplaces, twenty-foot-tall columned porches on both sides of the house, carved oaken doors, and a tower like a medieval castle. The wood-burning furnace in the house was so large that it could accommodate a full-size railroad tie. Broderick improved the property by building a log structure that served as his private Missouri Pacific Railroad stop at the bottom of the bluff so he could easily commute to St. Louis. He dubbed it Terrace Station. He built 385 steps up the bluff to his home and also built a pump house to bring Meramec River water up to the house. The stairs are overgrown now, and the riverside improvements are gone. Over the years, the turret has been removed from the structure, but it is still a very impressive home.

The majority of these later settlers were German immigrants. As many older residents recall, they were hard working, devout, and committed to education for their children. It has often been noted, too, that they "liked their beer," as did the other St. Louis German immigrants of the day. There were more taverns than any other type of business along Manchester Road, and there was a German school just over the Franklin County border. Many German families, such as the Dreinhofers, sent their sons there. This German influence

INTRODUCTION

top: Bill and Mary Kesselring are pictured in their combination store and bar. Next door to the establishment was Kesselring's Hall, where many local celebrations were held. This historic dance hall and community meeting place still stands on Old Manchester Road. Over the years, these buildings have also been known as Kesselring's Hall and Grove, the Wayside Inn, or the Pond Inn. Before the widespread use of air conditioning, picnic groves were the community meeting places, which is why there are so many towns with the name "Grove" incorporated into the name. Wedding dances, reunions, and other social gatherings were held at Kesselring's.

bottom: "This photo shows my uncle, George Poertner, and a group of his friends," said Bebe Poertner McKenzie, a longtime resident and history researcher. "They made beer in the barn, which is pictured right behind them. They called themselves 'the drinking club.' My grandma would not allow George to drink in the house or anywhere near the house, so he and his friends would go out into the pear orchard that was behind the house. There they could enjoy their beer in peace! " she added.
Pictured in the back row, left to right are: Oscar Hencken, George Dreitschen, Albert Muessemeyer, Henry Krueger, George Jordan, Charles Hessler, and George Poertner. In the front, left to right, are Joe Theiman, Gustav Grah, and Henry Beinke.

INTRODUCTION

top: The old Glencoe Train Station, now gone, stood at the end of Grand Avenue. The depot stood on a curve of the Meramec called "Rebel Bend," so named because Confederate soldiers were known to sneak past the Yankee's Home Guards here during the Civil War. This area has been an important crossroads since prehistoric times. The Crescent flint fields across the river drew Native Americans who used the flint for weapon points and other stone tools. At this point in the river, there has been a ford and a ferry through the years. "At times a boat was used to ferry people across from the farms (in Crescent) and one of the Lewis family members was the first station agent at the Glencoe depot, paddling back and forth across the river to work and home," said Al Foster, a St. Louis conservationist who researched this area in his 1983 report "Glencoe- from the beginning." A train robbery occurred here in 1910. Two thieves hid on the train and fired shots at the conductor and passengers. They disconnected the locomotive, the coal tender and the mail car from the rest of the train, then stole money from the mail car and chucked it into a cornfield to retrieve later. Some investigative work from the St. Louis Police nabbed both robbers and they were sent to the penitentiary in Jeff City. Foster notes that the last railroad track was removed from the Glencoe area in the 1970s. The railbed, now a multi-use trail, is named after Foster.

bottom: Centaur was once a bustling business area, processing lime and lumber for St. Louis markets. The depot at Centaur, pictured here, is gone now.

INTRODUCTION

top: William Kesselring, on left, is pictured with his bridge building crew. They built small cement bridges throughout the area in the 1930s and 1940s. Kesselring was a construction superintendent for the Willingham Company, a St. Louis firm that built schools and other commercial buildings.

right: Benjamin McDaniels (1844–1926) was born near Antire Road in Jefferson County and served in the Civil War. After the war, he came to the Glencoe area, where he was a worker in the limestone mining operations. A dollar a day was a typical wage in those days. Benjamin and his wife Elizabeth are buried in Bethel Cemetery. Many of their descendants remain in the area.

continued up to the 1930s, when the traditional year-end picnics for the old Pond School always started with a parade to Funk's Grove in Grover. There, a picnic under the grove featured a maypole, singing, and pageants. Large German bands were brought in from St. Louis, complete with tubas and lederhosen-clad musicians.

By the early 1850s, the Missouri Pacific Railroad line served southern Wildwood, giving residents an opportunity to travel to the city. On Wildwood's northern border, the Chicago, Rock Island, and Pacific Railroad came through the valley in the late 1870s, and the settlement of Monarch sprang up alongside it. Further west, the town of Centaur was also located on this line. The railroads brought industry

INTRODUCTION

top: "I have so many fond memories of the places we went in my Uncle John's truck. My Aunt Dora did her best to chaperone," recalls Dovie Berry. "The truck was filled with hay, and when night came, coal-oil lamps were lit. Someone was always blowing the lamps out and then they had to be re-lit. Aunt Dora would say, 'Ach! Children!' It's a wonder that the hay wasn't caught on fire!" she added. Pictured are members of the Gaehle, Krueger, Barnard, Kessels, Poertner, Lehmann, and Zinner families.

left: This maypole at Funk's Grove celebrated the end of the school year for Pond School students.

and jobs to the Wildwood area. Now, instead of farming, men could find jobs in the numerous clay mines, limestone quarries, or kilns scattered throughout our area. A large clay mine located just south of Manchester Road in what is now Rockwoods Reservation operated from 1856 to 1938.

One-room country schools were located every few miles so that students could easily walk. Also located every few miles were country stores that sold everything the residents needed: shoes, food, fabric, clothing, farm implements, and tools. Storekeepers would take eggs, milk, cream, garden produce, or butter as barter for their products.

INTRODUCTION

top: The Kreienkamp Store at 19160 Melrose Road is a rare example in St. Louis County of a rural store, and it is also the only surviving building associated with the failed town of Melrose. It was built around 1872. Originally leased by Herman Kreienkamp (1847–1924) and occupied by Louis Wackher, the postmaster, Kreienkamp operated the store himself from 1870 to 1873 before returning to farming. Emil J. Hardt ran the store for several years until Herman eventually bought the store on April 8, 1896. Herman Kreienkamp died in 1924. The store was taken over by his son Otto and Otto's wife Elizabeth Anna. Upon Otto's death in 1951 and Elizabeth's in 1970 their oldest son, Ralph Otto, and one of their daughters Mae Elizabeth ran the store until 1988 when it was sold. (Information courtesy of St. Louis County Department of Parks and Recreation in an inventory prepared by Esley Hamilton.)

right: An 1897 receipt from the Gaehle Store.

They would then exchange those products in the city for more merchandise. "When he was a child, my dad, Anton Schaedler, would sometimes ride into St. Louis with Herman Kreienkamp, who owned the Kreienkamp Store near us," recalled Wildwood resident Ervin Schaedler. "Some of the local guys had a standing order for gallon jugs of 905 Whisky. That was a common brand in those days. One day when Herman returned from his buying trip in the city, the guys were waiting for their orders. Herman said, 'Bad news, boys. The 905 has gone up to 35 cents a jug.' One old guy thought about it for a minute and then said, 'That's ok. I'd buy it even if it was 50 cents.'"

INTRODUCTION

This store, built in 1867 by Gustav Hoppenberg, once served the community of Orrville. Hoppenberg sold the store to Philip Fick in 1883. It is located at 526 Old Eatherton Road. One of the many rural hamlets that make up the current City of Wildwood, Orrville is located in a wooded valley at the intersections of Bonhomme Creek, Eatherton Road, and Orrville Road. Only a few buildings remain from the settlement.

John and Dora Gaehle owned a general store on Wild Horse Creek Road. Their large truck, dubbed the Wild Horse Creek Express, took farm products to the city and returned with merchandise to sell. "Uncle John would also use this truck to take everyone to county fairs and ball games," recalled Dovie Poertner Berry.

During the Depression, hard-up residents would not have been able to survive without the country storekeepers who gave them goods on credit. In addition to the general mercantiles, there were traveling peddlers. Many residents, including Dorothy Pendleton and Clifford Frazier, recall a Greek man named "Peddler Nick" who carried all of his merchandise in a huge pack on his back. "He walked from farm to farm on foot selling his wares," said Frazier. "It was so exciting when he came. We'd all gather around in the living room to see what he had in his pack," he added.

INTRODUCTION

top: This remarkable old photo shows a typical country store with the proprietor, Elmer Uhter, standing on the right. Uhter Store stood on Melrose Road. "We'd stop on our way to school and again on our way home, maybe to get a Baby Ruth candy bar," said Dorothy Pendleton, who went to school at Melrose. "It was a very small building—two rooms—and the whole place smelled like leather. He sold Weather Bird brand shoes. Mr. Uhter wore a flat cap and he had a little round tummy," she recalled.

bottom: The country store at 16952 Manchester Road, shown here, was renovated in the 1990s to become Wildwood's City Hall, and it remained in use by the city until recently. Frederick Rettker probably built this structure about 1879. At the time, it was the only general store in the immediate vicinity. Louis Fick bought the store in 1890 for two thousand dollars, and he was still the owner in 1911 when the telephone exchange was located in the building. Elmer Funk took ownership in 1921. The store and the adjoining picnic grove were important meeting places in the community.

Henry Frazier, his brother Grover, and their friend Daisy Jackson head off for an outing in their new automobile. Note the rutted dirt road. Passengers were expected to get out and push when roads were muddy!

Other Early Settlers

The advent of the automobile brought many changes. By the 1930s, people could drive or take the bus to the closest commercial shopping areas, which were in Maplewood or Wellston, and the country stores began to die out. The completion of a paved road from the city was a commercial pipeline for areas like Pond and Grover, and the population began a steady climb that continues today. A 1930s advertisement for the Big Chief restaurant coaxed city residents to give their eatery a try, boasting that their location was "only twenty-one miles from St. Louis, and paved all the way!"

Highway 109 was paved in the early 1930s, a portion of Highway 40 was built in the same decade, and other roadways were improved. A daily commute to the city now became feasible, and many people

INTRODUCTION

Designed for the automobile trade, the Big Chief Hotel in Wildwood was built in 1929, when Manchester Road formed part of the legendary U.S. Route 66 from about 1926 to 1932.
The Spanish Mission–style complex consisted of a restaurant and sixty-two cabins, each with its own garage. The cabins were laid out in a horseshoe pattern around the restaurant. Each cabin had two rooms, bunk beds, hot and cold running water, and steam heat. Cabins rented for $1.50 per night. Big Chief also had a twenty-four-hour gasoline service station.
Big Chief attracted tourists and St. Louisans that would take day trips out to Pond for lunch. Babe Ruth even visited Big Chief when the Yankees were in St. Louis.
After Route 66 was rerouted to Watson Road, business fell off, and the rooms were rented as efficiency apartments. The main building still stands at 17352 Old Manchester Road and is currently used as a restaurant. (From information courtesy of St. Louis County Department of Parks and Recreation in an inventory prepared by Esley Hamilton.)

took jobs in St. Louis. City residents could "motor" to the country for a picnic in Babler Park or a swim in the Meramec River. Many people had rustic weekend homes called "clubhouses" along the Meramec in towns like Sherman and Glencoe, and businesses sprang up to serve these new customers. A 1926 Bank of Eureka clerk, Pete Bienmuller, related that "each Monday the merchants from up to-

INTRODUCTION

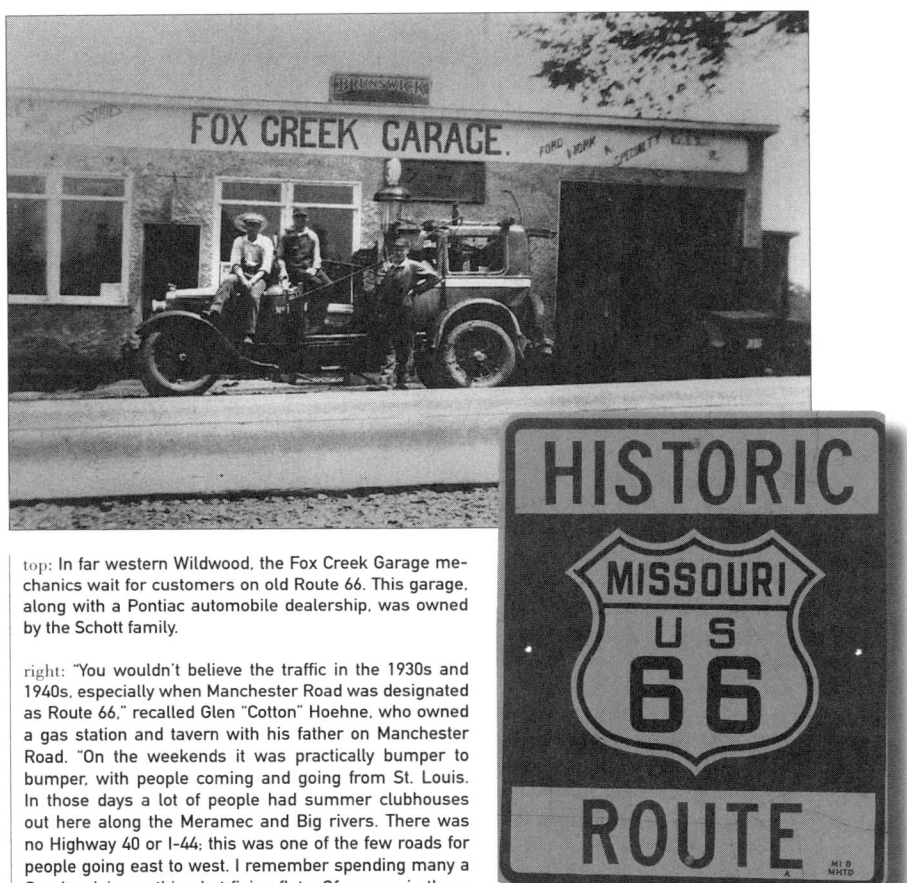

top: In far western Wildwood, the Fox Creek Garage mechanics wait for customers on old Route 66. This garage, along with a Pontiac automobile dealership, was owned by the Schott family.

right: "You wouldn't believe the traffic in the 1930s and 1940s, especially when Manchester Road was designated as Route 66," recalled Glen "Cotton" Hoehne, who owned a gas station and tavern with his father on Manchester Road. "On the weekends it was practically bumper to bumper, with people coming and going from St. Louis. In those days a lot of people had summer clubhouses out here along the Meramec and Big rivers. There was no Highway 40 or I-44; this was one of the few roads for people going east to west. I remember spending many a Sunday doing nothing but fixing flats. Of course, in those days nearly every car trip involved a flat tire.

"At my business, I built a big barbecue pit that would hold thirty slabs of ribs at a time. We were kept busy putting one slab of ribs after another on there. We sold barbecue like hot cakes—and our claim to fame was having the cleanest place and the coldest beer in West County."

ward Glencoe would deposit just stacks of money spent by people who came out on the old plug train for a day." These weekend visitors enjoyed the wide-open spaces and peaceful rural lifestyle. Many bought inexpensive building lots from local farmers and moved to "the country" permanently.

This Grover gas station, still standing, was located east of the current city hall on Manchester Road.

The Incorporation of Wildwood

The decades of the 1940s, 1950s, and 1960s were prosperous. The completion of Interstate 44 in 1962 made an easy commute for residents in the city, and more land was developed for housing. In the mid-1960s, the opening of the new Chrysler plant in Fenton offered jobs. Other St. Louis firms saw the trend and moved westward. The country schools were reorganized into one large district, and still the schools bulged at the seams. More schools were built. The growth continued as the St. Louis metropolitan area moved westward year by year. Cooper Bussman opened their Ellisville facility in 1979, and in the mid-1980s, Monsanto built their Life Sciences Research Center in Chesterfield, where many Wildwood residents work.

This growth was the driving force behind the creation of our town. Wildwood is a unique city because it did not evolve over time like most municipalities. Residents decided to take matters into their own hands, creating a town where they would have a say in how it was developed. In the 1980s, homebuilders began buying up large

INTRODUCTION

These two aerial photos show how the area around Grover has changed in the last fifty or sixty years. In the older photo at bottom, Manchester Road, then a gravel road, is running east to west in the middle of the picture; the view is looking south. The circled structures have the same roofline, both in the new map and the older map. Directly in the center on the south side of Manchester Road is the old Funk's Grove and store. At first it is hard to recognize as the city hall building that was used for many years, because it was enlarged with additions and dormers. The porch has been changed as well.

On the top right of the bottom photo is the baseball diamond that many longtime residents have mentioned. Even from the air, the worn spaces around the bases and pitcher's mound are visible. The Grover post office now covers that spot, and a new road and subdivision is located behind it. On the east side of Funk's Grove is Woods Road and just west of that is a gas station with a few cars; other than the gas station there are no cars visible, either on the roads or parked in driveways. Note the number of mature trees in the photo; many of the homes have backyard gardens visible as well. Most of these houses are still here. (Author's note: Many thanks to historian and cartographer Ron Kreienkamp for interpreting these maps!)

INTRODUCTION

Stovall's Grove, a historic tavern, was purchased in 1930 by George and Molly Stovall. Around 1935, the Stovalls' twin sons, Delbert and Delmer, founded a country and western band called the Missouri Valley Boys. Over the years, the band members have changed off and on, but it is believed that this is the oldest country and western band in Missouri. Delmer still plays with the band every Saturday night. Throughout the years, many music "notables" have played here on their road tours, including Brenda Lee, John Hartford, and Nix Nixon. The old-fashioned music hall has been updated and renovated recently, says principal owner Liz Elze. In addition to the bar, dance floor, and indoor areas, they have extensively renovated the patio under the sycamore grove, and the facility is available to rent for gatherings of all types.

tracts of land for housing developments, and local residents began attending public hearings at the St. Louis County Council. In 1987, residents learned that five hundred acres off Wild Horse Creek Road were designated to become a housing development of over seven hundred homes. About 150 residents gathered in the home of Maryanne Simmons, developing strategies and signing petitions to control the development.

More meetings led to a five-year incorporation effort, headed and funded solely by residents. Their efforts were met with a groundswell of support, both locally and throughout the county. Hundreds of volunteers worked on the effort, and St. Louis county songwriter and author Roger Taylor was inspired to write a song about feisty Wildwood residents fighting back against outside interests. Local lawyers like Dan Vogel and Eric Tremayne provided their pro-bono services to help the incorporation effort.

Schott's Garage.

In addition to the high-density subdivisions, residents opposed the proposed expansion of Route 109 into a six-lane divided highway designed to be an "outerbelt." The residents wanted to save as many trees as possible and control the number of houses allowed in each land parcel. Their battle cry was "Save the Greenbelt—Stop the Outerbelt." "The first 'incorporate Wildwood' meeting at Lafayette High School brought out five to six hundred people, and that was during a rain storm," said Sue Cullinane, an incorporation organizer who later served as council member and city administrator. She noted that the name "Wildwood" was a combination of Wild Horse and Rockwood.

The grassroots effort that started around kitchen tables ended up in the Missouri Supreme Court. The Court allowed the organizers of this community to place the question of creating a new city before the residents of the area now known as Wildwood. Boundaries were mandated; the new city borders should meet the borders of Chesterfield, Ellisville, and Eureka, with no "pockets" of land left over. The

INTRODUCTION

Wildwood city leaders at the incorporation on September 1, 1995.

western boundary was the Franklin County line. The resulting town is a whopper in size—sixty-seven square miles. Included in this area is twelve square miles of public land.

Don Kozlowski agreed to serve as the initial chairman of the incorporation effort, and twenty-five-hundred petition signatures were gathered to put the incorporation issue on the ballot. In 1995, voters overwhelmingly agreed to incorporate into a new city. On September 1, 1995, Wildwood was formed. Today, Wildwood continues that journey. Then as now, the city's main goal is "Planning Tomorrow Today." To ensure that its assets are retained, the city has created a planning process that supports all aspects of its government. This process ensures that future growth, development, and improvements will preserve the unique character of our community.

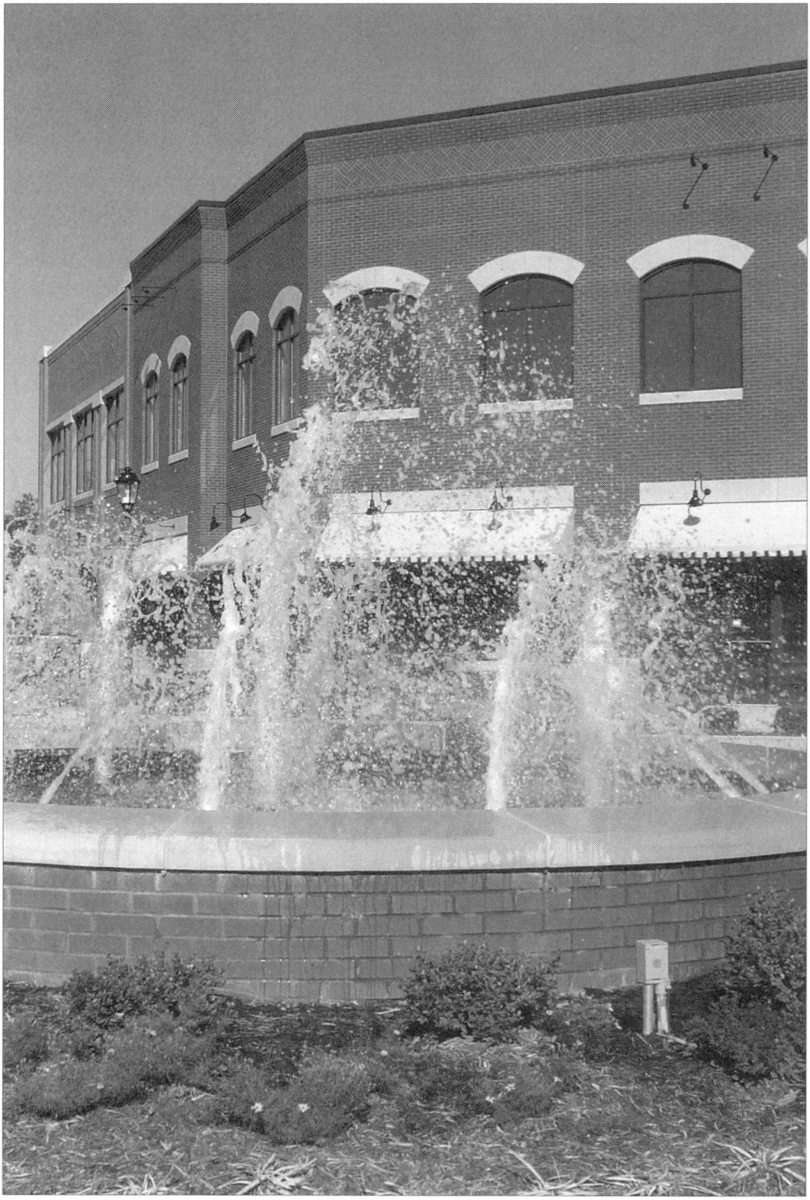

Chapter 1
THE CITY OF WILDWOOD

Less than two decades old, Wildwood has already seen many changes in its short history as an independent city. Some of the early leaders have moved on to other communities, but their ideas live on in the policies and procedures of local government. New residents have stepped into leadership roles, bringing new ideas and enthusiasm.

After the voters approved the incorporation, a ceremony was held at Babler State Park on September 1, 1995. The history of the area's small villages remains alive, but the newly formed city unified these formerly scattered developments and gave our area a new identity. From the beginnings of our new town, residents have enthusiastically supported the city by participation and attendance at festivals, concerts, recreation events, and parades. A demonstration of this unanimity is the popularity of "Wildwood Wear." Down the aisles of Dierberg's or Schnucks or in the booths at the local Rise and Dine, you can't go far without seeing a Wildwood t-shirt, polo, or cap! Before the creation of the city, the only community celebrations were at individual schools and churches. Now, there is always an occasion to celebrate our city.

Voters Embrace Wildwood
'We Were Right' About Development, Jubilant Backers Say
By Mark Schlinkmann
Regional Political Correspondent

Newly appointed city councilmen and women take the oath of office. Left to right: Bill Kennedy, Jim Wand, Charles Parsley, Kirk Miller, Dan Stegmann, Karen Owens, Jim Bellville, John Finley, Lisa Wax, John O'Shaughnessy, Ron Marcantano, Jeff Kochelek, Barb Foy, John Schroeder, Gerald Frank, and Charlotte Fink.

THE CITY OF WILDWOOD

top: The first city hall was originally a country store. From 1995 to 2008, city offices were housed at the renovated Funk's store on Old Manchester Road. At the end of 2008, Wildwood city offices moved to their new offices in the Wildwood Town Center, which is located at the intersection of Plaza Drive and Fountain Place. National City Bank is located on the first floor of this building and city welcoming offices are located on the first floor also. Other city offices are located on the second floor.

bottom: The new Wildwood City Hall. Photo courtesy of the City of Wildwood.

THE CITY OF WILDWOOD

top: Wildwood loves a parade! In this photo, Pond School parents and students exuberantly strut their stuff during the annual Wildwood Day parade. Pond School has a lot of reasons to show their "Pond Pride," since they have earned national distinction for their high test scores and other measures of school performance. They have been named on Missouri's "top ten" list, and they are the only school in Missouri to achieve the Blue Ribbon Award twice from the U.S. Department of Education. The state of Missouri's Gold Star School has been awarded to Pond on three occasions, more than any other elementary school in our state.

bottom: Patriotism is always in style in Wildwood. Here, a local Boy Scout and Cub Scout group march in an annual Wildwood Day parade. Boy Scout Troop 456 scouts have provided the reverential color guard and presentation of flags at every Wildwood Day event since 1995.

THE CITY OF WILDWOOD

top: A Wildwood treasure! This 1990s city council presentation honors the city's oldest resident, Emma Halbach Schlemper. She was 105 at the time; she is greatly missed. Pictured in the photo, left to right, are: Barb Foy, Dennis Corrigan, Lisa Wax, Gary Dueker, Maryanne Simmons, John Wild, Mike Narducci, Dennis Tacchi, John Schroeder, and Vern Hutson.

bottom: Babler Elementary Brownies in an early Wildwood Day parade. Scouting organizations are a big part of every Wildwood school..

City Staff

Administration Department

This department oversees the operation of city hall and deals with budgets, demographics, and sales tax rates. The city clerk's office handles voter registration, municipal records, election filings, and notary public services. They prepare, file, and distribute all city ordinances and resolutions.

Within the sixty-seven square miles of Wildwood's borders, there are seven zip codes! These zip codes are the remnants of the smaller towns that existed before the creation of Wildwood. City officials and residents have questioned the postal service about why there are so many zip codes, but apparently the assigning of zip codes is a complicated process, and existing codes are not easily changed. So that's why there is a Grover Post Office and a Glencoe Post Office, but no Wildwood Post Office.

Director of Planning and Parks

This is the department to see if you have questions about building permits, zoning, variances, code enforcement, historic structures, trustee information, subdivision process, GIS and mapping, or the town center project.

Public Works Department

The Public Works Department oversees the maintenance of city infrastructure. In addition, the department handles trash and recycling contracts, special event permits, inspections and tree trimming.

Municipal Court

There are two court dates per month at Wildwood City Hall. For more information, call (636)458-8277.

THE CITY OF WILDWOOD

Wildwood City Council: Front row, left to right: Jean Vedvig, Patricia Thibeault, Tammy Shea, Mayor Tim Woerther, David Sewell, Susan Baker. Back row, left to right: Tony Salvatore, Jim Baugus, Bart Cohn, Holly Parks, Rick Wise, Bruce Colella, Nick Roppollo, Holly Ferris, Ron James. Not pictured: Michele R. Bauer.

Wildwood Town Center

In 1996, the City of Wildwood adopted a comprehensive master plan to provide a roadmap for the future growth of the entire community. A key element of that plan was the designation of a new town center. The intent of this designation was to provide the community with a "hometown" environment where people could live, work, and play. Planners felt that it would also provide the city with a focal point and stronger sense of community identity.

Many local residents were involved in the town center planning process. As of 2009, the development is well underway. There is a Dierberg's, Walgreen's drugstore, and an assortment of banks, shops, restaurants, and offices. The new Wildwood Hotel opened in 2008. A unified building style is found throughout the development, using stone with brick for an elegant look. Many community celebrations such as music concerts and movie nights are held in the new town center.

From the beginning, the city leaders and residents wanted the new area to be a community gathering place. With that in mind, a great deal of thought has gone into the aesthetic appeal and ambiance of the development. Bike trails, wide sidewalks, and walking paths are included in the design. Several eateries have outside tables where diners can enjoy the charming touches that have been included in the development. A handsome clock tower, brick and stone street signage, upscale lighting fixtures, pergolas with climbing vines, benches, fountains, flowers, and foliage are thoughtful touches that encourage residents to relax and enjoy their visit there.

THE CITY OF WILDWOOD

Anniversary Park

Chapter 2
RECREATION

Wildwood residents have always worked hard, but they take recreation just as seriously! All it takes is a glance at a Wildwood map to see that natural areas fill up a good percentage of our sixty-seven square miles. Two state parks, a county park, and a number of city parks are available for outdoor fun and sports. Hiking trails, hunting and shooting ranges, equestrian areas, and two rivers for fishing or canoeing are just a few of the great amenities to be found here. Less than thirty minutes away, St. Louis offers a free zoo, major league sporting events, museums, symphony, theatres, and other cultural attractions. From the earliest settlers with their church socials to the youth sports leagues of today, residents know it's those "just-for-kicks" activities that make life enjoyable.

RECREATION

"Town Team" Baseball

The era of town team baseball is represented in this group of photos taken in the 1940s. After a long day of putting up hay or working in the city, men would hustle home, clean up, put on their uniforms, and head to the diamond. Many men continued playing throughout adulthood. Ball games were well-attended community events; cars would pull up around the diamond, with beer and soda on ice in the back seat or a flask under the driver's seat. A box of mom's chicken, carefully fried and nestled in an oatmeal box lined with newspaper, made a great picnic while the family watched the game. If a ball put a dent in your hood or broke a car window, well, that was just too bad. Nobody sued in those days. Little kids perched on the big fat fenders of their parents cars, waiting for an opportunity to chase foul balls through cornfields and hay pastures. "We made a ball field next to Funk's Grove, where the Grover Post Office is now," recalled Ray Athey. "We also made a ball diamond just west of Pond, where the Rockwoods Reservation pine thicket is now," he added. Another diamond was located on Highway 109 near the Old State Road intersection.

"Town team ball was BIG when I was a kid," said Bob Leiweke. "Every little town had their own team. The places where we played were often-times just a cow pasture. We'd throw off the cow chips and drag the field to smooth it out. Our team wasn't really an organized deal; we were just a bunch of country boys who wanted to play ball. We elected one of the older guys to be our captain. He'd go out and get us sponsors to buy our uniforms. We played teams from Eureka, Glencoe, Sherman, Jedburgh, and other towns around the area. Were we any good? You bet! We were all good players," he laughed.

RECREATION

top: Glencoe baseball team with scorekeeper, 1940s. Back row, left to right: Johnnie Miller, Jim Miller, Al Heinz, Hubert Leuthauser, Jimmy Knox, Al McKinnon, Clement Hatz, Clarence "Shorty" Rickard. Front row: Andy Andereck, ____ Rupp, Warren "Bud" Jaeger, John Harness, Roy Jaeger, and Charles Krieg. Scorekeeper Marcella Harness is in front.

bottom: This town team was comprised of young men from the Wildwood area. Their home diamond was just across Highway 109 from the La Salle Brothers property at Glencoe. Note the mismatched uniforms. This photo was taken just after World War II, so players wore whatever uniforms they could find, from Melrose, Glencoe, Chesterfield, or Grover. Players, back row, left to right: John Harness, Harry Bacon, Virgil Rickard, Dominic Ross. Middle row: Bud Rickard, Ray Athey, Harry Paffrath, Roy Athey. Front row: "Scrub" Rickard, Dick Jaeger, Hicks Jaeger, "Shorty" Rickard. The bat boy in the front row is Wayne Rambaud.

opposite top right: Grover baseball team, 1940–41. Members were Norman "Bud" Rickard, Roy Athey, Henry "Bill" Bopp, Vernon Paubel, Gilbert Reinke, Bill Steinbrueck, Vic Reinke, Earl Straub, Jimmy Koch, and Ray Athey.

RECREATION

Al Foster Trail

The development of this natural area was a cooperative effort. "Much of the park land along the river was acquired before the incorporation of Wildwood," said Ron Coleman, executive director of the Open Space Council. He noted that the Meramec River Recreation Association (MRRA) met in the 1970s, 1980s, and 1990s, planning the best use of the abandoned railway bed that was once used by the Missouri Pacific Railroad. This group, along with the Missouri Division of State Parks, the Open Space Council, the Great Rivers Greenways District (GRGD), the City of Wildwood, and St. Louis County government all worked together to acquire the land and develop the trail. Starting in the 1970s, Operation Clean Stream, an extension of the Open Space Council, organized volunteers to clean up the area and many partnering organizations also helped with the cleanup effort. "It's been a good partnership," said Coleman. Before the development of the trail, this was a rough area frequented by off-roaders and partiers. Cement block buildings and other debris left from a sand and aggregate dredging operation were torn down and removed. A huge dredging barge, however, still remains, half submerged, in the river along the trail. It makes a good home for fish and the riverside animals that live along the Meramec. At Sherman Beach, there is a narrow path that leads down to the river. There is a lovely view of the sandbar, a railroad trestle, and the river. Parking is available

Photo by Carol Pope

Photo by David Lickerman

on either end of the trail. The trailhead parking lot is at the intersection of Grand and Third streets in downtown Glencoe. Call (314)615-7275 for more information, or visit www.stlouisco.com/parks.

A new trail addition to the park system is coming in the summer of 2009. The Rock Hollow Trail will be built on what is locally referred to as "The Zombie Road." This abandoned road, once named Lawler Ford Road, is now a rutted track, which runs from near Ridge Meadows Elementary to the Al Foster Trail, a distance of two to three miles. "This road used to be a hauling road for the mining operations in the area," Coleman noted. The road will be turned into a modern hiking and biking trail. It's not clear why the road is nicknamed Zombie. Ghost hunters and paranormal groups maintain that there are supernatural forces there and they cite a number of deaths, suicides, and unusual events. A more plausible explanation is that there was once a resident who lived in the area with a nickname of Zombie. The "spooky" reputation of the road will undoubtedly make it a popular trail.

Babler State Park

This huge park offers recreation for everyone, including equestrians, hikers, campers, and bikers. A variety of pavilions and shelters has made Babler a site for reunions and picnics for generations. In 1937, Jacob L. Babler donated 2,441 acres for the park. He named the park in honor of his brother, Edmund L. Babler, a prominent St. Louis surgeon.

The park has a stable, youth camping areas, and a visitor center that

A statue commemorating Edmund Babler is prominently featured in the park.

showcases some of the wildlife that is found in the park. Another feature is the Jacob Babler Outdoor Education Center, which has cabins, a dining hall, a recreation hall, and a pool. Community festivals like Wildwood Day were held here in the past, and an extensive summer camp for youth remains as a popular annual activity. Because the park is so close to the St. Louis area it is well used and is certainly one of Wildwood's most cherished assets. The park is located at 800 Guy Park Drive, Wildwood, MO 63005. Its phone number is (636)458-3813.

RECREATION

top: Horses wait for their turn to hit the trail. Babler Park's stables and trails make it a favorite with equestrians.

bottom: The Colemans were early Wildwood pioneers. Their family cemetery is located near the Babler Park stables.

Civilian Conservation Corps

Evidence of the Civilian Conservation Corps' (CCC) work in the 1930s is evident throughout Babler State Park in Wildwood. The CCC lived and worked here. "It was a godforsaken wilderness then, just nothing but trees," said Kirkwood resident Paul Ward, who served at Babler Park with "The Corps." "I was brought out here from St. Louis on a flatbed truck, and for a while, we stayed in tents, until they built dormitories."

Young men serving in the military-style, New Deal program were paid twenty-five dollars a month, with twenty dollars of that going to their families, who were hard pressed to survive during the Depression. "We had to work to spend the five dollars that we were given," said Ward. "There was nothing to spend it on. Sometimes we walked all the way to Chesterfield, just to buy a soda."

Paul Ward (1917–2002) with his CCC overalls. Courtesy *Webster-Kirkwood Times.*

Stone bridges, gates and walls, rustic buildings, roads, walkways, and more still remain as evidence of their work. Native stone and timber were used to keep building costs low. "There are still some concrete foundations where our camp was—in the valley just north of the swimming pool," said Earl Wilson, an Olivette resident.

"You know those huge stones at the entrance of the park? Well, I had a hand in getting those down there. There were no roads then—it took three or four half-ton Dodge trucks that we used, along with a four-wheel flatbed hauler, to get them from the quarry down to the entrance of the park. We used a winch and big pieces of pipe for rollers," he recalled. "We also brought stone from the quarry, and the men would lay the stones in the roadbed by hand, then we'd dump on chat (a filling material) to fill in the gaps."

"When I came here from 1937 to 1939, I thought it was so beautiful, so peaceful, and such a change from St. Louis, where I grew up," said Wilson. "This park and my Corps service changed the course of my life. I still come out here quite often, you know, just to get away from the noise and the hustle of the city," he added.

Earl Wilson (1917–2008) outside the Nature Center in Babler. Courtesy *Webster-Kirkwood Times*.

RECREATION

top: The Babler Park stable displays the traditional look of a CCC structure.

bottom: This stone bridge was built by the young men of the CCC in the 1930s.

RECREATION

Greensfelder Park

The land that is now Greensfelder Park has been used for logging and mining in the past. Missouri's Conservation Commission acquired part of the property for Rockwoods Reservation, which adjoins Greensfelder Park. Originally called Rockwood Park, the park was officially renamed in September of 1965.

Area residents owe a big thank you to A. P. Greensfelder, who was born in St. Louis in 1879. Thanks to his generosity and vision, we have this wonderful green space to enjoy. In 1963, the St. Louis Regional Planning and Construction Foundation, which Greensfelder established in 1939, donated the land that is now Greensfelder Park. It is administered by St. Louis County Parks.

This 1,724-acre park, flanking both sides of Allenton–Six Flags Road, has shaded hiking and biking trails, equestrian and group camping, a nature center, picnic shelters, and playgrounds. Equestrians love Greensfelder for its horse boarding facility, equestrian trails, camp sites, and show ring area. Four shelters may be reserved for groups. Their mailing address is 4515 Hencken Road, Wildwood, MO 63069. For more information about camping at Greensfelder, call (314)615-4FUN. For information about their hayrides, call (314)615-4386.

Photo by Carol Pope

RECREATION

Hidden Valley Ski and Golf Resort

Hidden Valley is a year-round recreational facility unlike any other in the St. Louis area. During the winter months, Hidden Valley is dedicated to downhill skiing and is open to the public. Lessons and a complete ski rental shop are available. Located in southern Wildwood, the resort commands a wonderful view of the Meramec Valley. Hidden Valley owner Tim Boyd was skiing in California thirty years ago when he realized that you don't necessarily have to have a mountain to go skiing—you only have to have a good steep Missouri hill. Local farmers had known for years that the Hidden Valley property was too hilly to farm, and so it was used as a chicken ranch. This is the ski resort's twenty-sixth season. They will be adding snow tubing to their activities this year. Hidden Valley is located off Alt Road at 17409 Hidden Valley Drive. Visit their website at hiddenvalleyski.com or call their office at (636)938-5373.

RECREATION

RECREATION

Anniversary Park

This well-used thirteen-acre park is strategically located at 16511 Clayton Road. The property borders Caulks Creek and a small shopping area at the intersection of Strecker and Clayton roads. This park honors the tenth anniversary of the founding of Wildwood, and it was completed in April of 2006. Along with a lovely pavilion, there is a playground, benches, restrooms, a multiple-use court with basketball hoops, and a drinking fountain. The parking area is adjacent.

RECREATION

Wildwood Planning and Parks Department

The City of Wildwood's Department of Planning and Parks is charged with implementation of the city's park plans. They develop and maintain all of the city parks and miles of multiple-use trails. Another aspect of their work is to offer a variety of recreational programs for city residents, from Easter Egg hunts for toddlers to scrapbooking classes for adults. Over the years, they have sponsored many events that encourage residents to stay active. Some examples of these are the annual "Cabin Fever Hike," "National Trails Day," and the "Route 66 5K Run/Walk." These well-loved events not only help residents stay fit, but they also show residents the wide variety of programs in the Wildwood area.

Wildwood's Parks and Recreation Department sponsors many events for city residents. Annually, they sponsor walk/run competitions, hikes, egg hunts, special interest classes, concerts, movie nights, and more.

Pond Athletic Association

The Pond Athletic Association, a not-for-profit corporation, was incorporated on May 21, 1963. Their mission is to promote youth sports. The founders of the association were Curtis Glore, Jr., Fred Waterhouse, III, W. C. Bockstiegel, Earl Bartman, Wm. E. Steinbruesck, and Allen B. Hughes.

In the last forty years, the group has grown in size, and their work has impacted the lives of thousands of area youth. As of 2008, the association has over nine hundred member families enrolled, and they serve over two thousand area youngsters every year. Pond Athletic Association is located on Pond Road just north of Highway 100. They have seven well-maintained diamonds, asphalt parking areas, a concession stand, and an abundance of shade trees. They offer training in baseball for youth ages five through eighteen.

Pond School Park

Pond School Park stands as a monument to the dedication of many local residents to save the historic old school and return it to usefulness.

This one-acre property was donated to the community in the 1800s by the Dreinhofer family with the stipulation that the land be used for a school. The Dreinhofer farm was adjacent to the west and the white-frame old farmhouse is still standing on Manchester Road.

There have been four structures in this neighborhood named Pond School. The first known school was built near the intersection of Pond and Manchester roads. From all estimates, sometime around 1880, the second school was constructed on the land that the Dreinhofers had donated. This wooden schoolhouse caught fire sometime after the turn of the century, and it burned to the ground. Around 1914, a new school featured many modern improvements over the original wooden schoolhouse. The structure was constructed primarily of concrete, clay, and stucco—three components known for their strength and fireproofing capabilities.

The new schoolhouse was constructed directly in front of the burned-out site of the second school. Dovie Berry, Barney Gaehle, Roy Athey, Frances Poe, and others all recall that there was a family crypt behind the school. This was located where the grassy area of the park is now. There were bones in the crypt, and it was a common schoolyard challenge to go into the crypt on a dare from classmates. The burial place was moved in later years.

The Pond School was active throughout the first half of the twentieth century. It was operational when Manchester Road was improved and renamed Route 66 in 1926.

RECREATION

| This rear view of the school shows the playground and the Ronald W. James Pavilion.

With the reorganization and consolidation of the area school districts in the 1950s, a decision was made to construct a new Pond School just west and within sight of the old school. This school is still in operation today as an elementary school, administered by the Rockwood School District.

After the children for the old Pond School transferred to the new school, the school district utilized the old schoolhouse as a school for children with special needs. This special school would last for over a decade, at which time the school district also constructed administrative offices in the old schoolhouse around 1970.

These administrative offices would occupy the Pond School for some years, at which time the school began to fall into serious disrepair from maintenance neglect. It was only used for equipment storage then.

Around 1998, a group of concerned citizens approached the Rockwood School District about saving the building and restoring it for a small museum. In 1999, the school property was returned to a Dreinhofer descendant, Mrs. Lorraine Conreux, since the school was no

This fine stone wall along Manchester Road defines the front boundary of the newly restored Pond School Park. The wall was constructed by workers from the WPA in the 1930s.

longer being used for educational purposes. Many local citizens and Wildwood staff members worked on school restoration effort and park development.

Towering shade trees are a fine asset of this lovely park. Amenities at the park include a playground, picnic area, and a beautiful pavilion, dedicated as the Ronald W. James Pavilion. Mr. James is a longtime city council member and Boy Scout leader who was recognized for his years of community service to the citizens of Wildwood.

The restored school has a stucco exterior and handsome period details such as copper gutters, reproduction light fixtures, and a red tile roof. Red paving bricks in the rear of the school bears the names of many citizens who donated money to fund the restoration. The city has used the park for their summer concerts and other events. The pavilion and school building are both used for meetings and gatherings of all types. Rentals may be arranged by calling the City of Wildwood at (636)458-0440.

RECREATION

Wabash, Frisco, and Pacific Railroad

This twelve-inch gauge railroad, operated by a dedicated team of railroad enthusiasts, is open every Sunday, May through October.

The thirty-minute ride is a two-mile round trip that travels along the scenic Meramec River beside the Al Foster Trail in southern Wildwood. Tall palisades of limestone, views of wildlife, and woodlands make this a memorable trip for adults as well as children.

The WF&P Railway organization was originally formed in 1939, when a group of railway enthusiasts acquired a twelve-inch gauge steam locomotive (Engine #171) and the use of a thirty-acre estate located on the southeast corner of Brown Road and Natural Bridge in St. Louis. They relocated to their present site in 1961.

For more information, visit their website at www.wfprr.com or call (636)587-3538.

Photo by Carol Pope

RECREATION

Rockwoods Reservation

Rockwoods Reservation, a state forest and wildlife refuge in Wildwood, celebrated its seventieth year in 2008. Its establishment in 1938 was made possible through the efforts of a group of St. Louis businessman, including A. P. Greensfelder. Other gifts and purchases have increased the park to its present size of 1,898 acres.

The park has had a fascinating history. In 1803, Ninian Hamilton received a Spanish land grant and started a mill and a small farm here with his family. Hamilton Creek, which flows through Rockwoods, is named after him. Later, the land was used for clear-cut logging by the Woods-Christy Lumber Company. In 1857, they subdivided the now-bare ground and tried to sell lots for a subdivision, but the enterprise failed. Next, the land passed into the hands of the Cobb-Wright-Case Mining Company, and limestone mining was begun.

This well-loved "Smokey" on Highway 109 greets thousands of area residents each day as they travel past Rockwoods Reservation.

Rockwood Reservation Visitor Center.

An old kiln from the limestone-mining era is along the main road leading to the visitor center. This valley was once a bustling company town, with a company store, post office, school, boarding house, small-gauge railroad, and two dozen homes for the workers. In all, about one hundred people lived in the town. Across from the spring is a private home, the only complete structure that remains from the Glencoe Lime Company era. In 1938, the land passed to the Missouri Conservation Commission.

Rockwoods is a diverse park, with springs, rock formations, a prairie, caves, hiking trails, picnic areas, forests, and evidence of past uses of the land. The park is managed by the Missouri Department of Conservation. It is located at 2751 Glencoe Road, just off Highway 109. For more information, call the visitor center at (636)458-2236.

RECREATION

Six Flags St. Louis

Six Flags St. Louis has eight theme sections, numerous shows, restaurants, games, and shops as well as seven roller coasters including The Boss, Mr. Freeze, Batman The Ride, and The Screamin' Eagle, which once held the Guinness Book of World Records title of Longest, Tallest, Fastest Wooden Roller Coaster. The twelve-acre Hurricane Harbor water park offers slides, wave pool, and a kids area. The park is located at the intersection of I-44 and Allenton–Six Flags Road in Eureka.

Six Flags chose this area because the 1960 census figures showed a large population within five hundred miles of Eureka. The land where Six Flags is now located was once a farm and right across the road from the park, where the Holiday Inn is now located, was the home of the St. Louis County Poor Farm for a time. Local steam-power enthusiasts hosted threshing demonstrations on the farm for several years in the 1960s. Farmer Will Eakin sold his land in the 1960s, and it was divided into several parcels, according to Jan Long of Long Ford, which is just south of the theme park. "At the time Six Flags came, this area was unincorporated St. Louis County," she added. After Six Flags bought the property and began building the theme park, the City of Eureka and the City of Pacific sparred over the annexation of the Allenton area. Both wanted to annex it, but residents voted both down. Later, the area was annexed into the City of Eureka. For more information, call the park at (636)938-4800 or visit their website at www.sixflags.com.

The West County Lion's Club. This fun-loving civic group, whose members are pictured here in 2003, is open to all West County men who want to socialize and make a difference in their community. Like all Lion's Clubs, their focus is on healthy sight. They collect eyeglasses for distribution all over the world, and they host barbeque dinners to raise money for their projects. An annual event is the benefit bowling tournament in Ellisville. As a result of their hard work, they are able to offer scholarships every year to Eureka High School students. In addition to contributing $10,000 each year to Lion's eye research, the group hosts vision screenings and gives emergency help in the community when needed.

Chapter 3
COMMUNITY ORGANIZATIONS

Wildwood residents of all ages can stay as busy as they like, with a wide range of activities, including sports clubs, civic-minded groups, school PTOs, and booster organizations for sport teams. Some examples can be found in this section. Newcomers will find that this is the best way to settle into their new community and make a difference in our town's quality of life.

Eureka's Volunteer Fire Department serves southern Wildwood. Pictured here are some early firefighters, along with their helpers: Left to right: Dan Wallach, Jack Davis (flanked by his twin sons Bill and Bob) Fred Arnold, and Walter Dempsey.

Eureka Volunteer Fire Department

The Eureka Volunteer Fire Department was formed after a major fire destroyed a large section of the downtown area of Eureka in the 1950s. In 1970, a referendum was placed on the ballot, and the voters approved the creation of a tax-supported fire district. The district currently has three firehouses. In addition to fighting fires and handling emergency medical responses, Eureka Fire District personnel are involved with community education, emergency medical services, and disaster preparedness programs. CPR and first aid classes are conducted monthly, and tours of the engine houses are always welcome. For non-emergencies, call (636)938-5505.

| Ever ready, the Eureka Fire Department serves residents in southern portions of Wildwood.

COMMUNITY ORGANIZATIONS

Metro West Fire Protection District

The Metro West Fire Protection District was formed in 1934. It provides service to all or portions of Ballwin, Chesterfield, Clarkson Valley, Castlewood, Ellisville, Sherman, Wildwood, Winchester, and unincorporated St. Louis County.

Metro West operates out of five firehouses in Wildwood, Ballwin, Castlewood, and Ellisville. These stations are spread throughout the 57.5-square-mile district, allowing them to rapidly respond to all community emergencies. Administrative offices for the district are located in Wildwood at 17065 Manchester Road.

| An aerial photo of the Metro West Fire Department.

COMMUNITY ORGANIZATIONS

Monarch Fire Protection District

This fire district began in 1925, when local businessmen decided to form a fire district. At first they were located in Bellefontaine Motors, near the intersection of Olive Street and Chesterfield Parkway East. They sold fire tags that were affixed to the outside of houses for three dollars per year, and they also raised funds by hosting yearly picnics.

Currently, the district has 120 employees and covers 55 square miles and services more than 60,000 people living in the cities of Ballwin, Chesterfield, Clarkson Valley, Creve Coeur, Maryland Heights, Wildwood, and unincorporated St. Louis County. Last year, the district responded to over 5,300 calls for help. For more information call (314)514-0900.

St. Louis County Police— Wildwood Precinct

St. Louis County Police Department has a contract with the city to provide police service for area residents. Twenty-one officers, a precinct captain, a lieutenant, and three sergeants are assigned to the Wildwood Precinct located at the Metro West Firehouse at 17065 Manchester Road. In addition, two neighborhood policing officers and a traffic officer are also assigned to the precinct. Four school resource officers are located at Lafayette High, La Salle Springs Middle, Rockwood Valley Middle, and Wildwood Middle schools.

In addition to the 29 police officers permanently assigned to the Wildwood Precinct, over 750 commissioned police officers on the St. Louis County Police Department are readily available to address any major police concern that could develop. Detectives with the St. Louis County Division of Criminal Investigation conduct investigations of felony crimes or any situation as requested by the Wildwood supervisors. All police-related resources available to the St. Louis County Police Department are available to the City of Wildwood. For more information call (636)458-9194.

Until 1955, law enforcement for the Wildwood area was provided by the St. Louis County Sheriff's office. During the week, there was very little need of police services, and residents would call a central dispatcher in the case of emergencies.

Deputies like Charlie St. Onge, George Gaehle, Gilbert Poertner, and Allie Laupp were local men hired by the Sheriff's office to keep the peace on weekends.

"They would go around to the dance halls to break up fights, that sort of thing," recalled Rusty Pendleton. "I remember that Allie Laupp was a quiet sort of guy; he had a hard time catching anyone, because he refused to go over thirty miles per hour." Another local lawman of a different sort is remembered by many older residents. "Joe Feco was not a very big guy, but I'll tell you, he was fearless," remembers Pendleton. "He would just take out after anybody, no matter what. One time in the 1950s there was an incident that shows what Joe was made of. He'd just been given a new squad car, and it was equipped with a radio. He got a call that there was a robber escaping down towards Eureka, and he took off like a shot. With the radio he knew where the guy was going, so he parked his squad car sideways, there on the main road that came from the east into Eureka. This was before they put in Interstate 44; all of the roads were just two-lane then, of course. He laid across the hood and when the robber came, Joe blasted away at him. The robber plowed right into Joe's squad car, going sixty-seventy miles an hour, and of course Joe was thrown off and hurt really bad. The squad car was totaled and Joe was in the hospital for a long time, but he got the crook. That's just the kind of guy Joe was. He was the biggest little man around."

COMMUNITY ORGANIZATIONS

An early Wildwood deputy, Charlie St. Onge, is pictured here on his motorcycle. On the left is his friend Henry Krueger.

La Salle Institute

The La Salle Institute, located just off Highway 109 in Wildwood, was founded in 1872. The La Salle Christian Brothers are a Roman Catholic congregation of religious men.

Ninian Hamilton, an early settler, acquired the hilltop property from a Spanish land grant in 1803. Over the years, this building has served as an orphanage, a Catholic high school, a seminary, and a home for retired clergy. Before the Catholic parishes of St. Alban Roe and Sacred Heart in Eureka were established, many local residents came to La Salle for weekly masses.

Throughout its early history, the clear-running "La Salle Spring" nearby provided the complex with good water. Due to safety concerns, the reservoir has been filled in. When a portion of the land was sold to Rockwood School District in the early 1990s, the waterway was channeled underground, but the spring still runs and gives its name to the nearby La Salle Springs Middle School.

| This old postcard shows the chapel at La Salle.

COMMUNITY ORGANIZATIONS

top: Many retreats and conferences are held at La Salle Institute.

bottom: A peaceful cemetery and grotto behind the center is the resting place for many St. Louis–area priests and brothers.

Marianist Retreat Center

The Marianist Retreat Center in southern Wildwood is a historically notable site. It is also a very beautiful property, situated as it is with hilltop views of the Glencoe valley and the Meramec River. The original home on the property, called Marycliff, was built in 1891 by Alfred Carr, an executive with the Missouri-Pacific Railroad Company, and Angelica Yeatman Carr, daughter of notable St. Louisan James E. Yeatman. Angelica Carr's family spent part of the year in a home just across the valley, in what is now Radcliffe Subdivision.

In 1896, the house was passed to the Carrs' son, Peyton, and his wife, Josephine Kehlor. It was used as a summer home for many years, as was common with wealthy St. Louis families in the days before air conditioning. The Glencoe train station made it easy for them to escape the city heat and travel to their cool, shady country estate. In 1943, the family sold the property to the Brewers' and Maltsters' Benevolent Association for use as a clubhouse.

In 1950, the property changed hands again, this time being bought by the Society of Mary. This property has a little bit of hidden history. Many years ago, one of the religious brothers related that there were a number of classical Roman statues in the gardens when the society purchased the property. After some discussion, it was decided to destroy the unclad statues. They are buried in the garden. The 120-acre complex includes a chapel, lodging, and conference facilities that are used year round for retreats and other functions. The center is located at 4000 Highway 109. For more information call (636)938-5390 or visit their website at www.mretreat.org.

COMMUNITY ORGANIZATIONS

West St. Louis County Chamber of Commerce

The West St. Louis County Chamber of Commerce is a not-for-profit membership organization of businesses and professional people. Members work together to promote the growth and expansion of commerce in the West St. Louis County area. The fifty-one-year-old association represents businesses and the community in eight cities, including Ballwin, Clarkson Valley, Ellisville, Manchester, Twin Oaks, Valley Park, Wildwood, Winchester, and unincorporated St. Louis County. They are located at 134 Enchanted Parkway in Manchester. Their phone number is (636)230-9900. For more information, see their website, www.westcountychamber.com.

| West County Chamber of Commerce.

Wyman Center

This historic camp in southern Wildwood got its start in 1897 by serving as a summer retreat for St. Louis–area children. Trains first brought the youngsters to the depot in Eureka, where they were picked up and transported to the farm with horses and wagons. Later, buses picked up the kids at specified locations in the city. One mother was assigned to each cabin of children. The goal of the camp founders was to send each "tenement child" home several pounds heavier, with color in their cheeks from healthy outdoor activities and plenty of nutritious food. From those small beginnings, Camp Wyman, now called Wyman, has grown to become a nationally and internationally recognized leader in innovative youth programs. In all, there are approximately 250 acres and 40 buildings on the Wyman site, including dormitories, a chapel, a laundry, post office, and a spacious dining hall. They are located at 600 Kiwanis Drive, at the end of Forby Road. For more information about Wyman, call (636)938-5245 or visit their website at www.wymancenter.org.

This early camp photo shows children outside of the cabins. A number of the old buildings survive from the early days of the center. Some of the buildings were brought here from the 1904 World's Fair.

COMMUNITY ORGANIZATIONS

Transporting children from the Eureka train depot to the camp.

COMMUNITY ORGANIZATIONS

The Wildwood Family YMCA

Former mayor Ron Marcantano had a hand in getting our local YMCA branch location. He was acquainted with the YMCA director, and he heard that the YMCA was thinking of a new branch location in West County. "Why not Wildwood?" Marcantano asked. He invited the YMCA director to come on a driving tour of the area, and they liked the Highway 109 location. The Wildwood Family YMCA, 2641 Highway 109, opened its doors in 2001 with a warm embrace from the community, right from the start. It offers a friendly, supportive atmosphere for kids, teens, families, and active older adults. The YMCA is a not-for-profit organization all with a mission of building healthy spirits, bodies, and minds for all. The Wildwood facility features an indoor pool with a two-story water slide, wellness center with group cycling and free-weight areas, gymnasium, indoor track, steam rooms, locker and family change rooms. Programs include swim classes, exercise classes, camps, and sports. The Wildwood Family YMCA partners with many other community organizations and is volunteer based. It is open to all, regardless of their ability to pay. To learn more, visit ymcastlouis.org/wildwood or call (636)458-6636.

COMMUNITY ORGANIZATIONS

The Garden Society of Wildwood

This group gets together the second Monday of every month to visit various gardens and nurseries. They also have guest speakers on many topics, including wildlife conservation and co-existing with local wildlife, landscaping, water gardening, and other topics. They share information and plants, have craft sessions relating to plants, and they volunteer their time to beautify the community. "Most of all we bring people together who appreciate gardening and are willing to share their lives with other people with similar interests," said society member Ruth Foster. The group welcomes new members. If you are interested in joining, contact Julie Housley at (314)518-7759.

Wildwood Garden Society members during a work session at Bethesda Retirement Home on Old State Road.

The Wildwood Historical Society

The Wildwood Historical Society was founded in 1999 to continue the work of the Wildwood Historical Preservation Committee. Meetings are held at Bethel United Methodist Church at 7:00 p.m. on the third Tuesday of each month.

The Society's Mission Statement

The purpose of the Wildwood Historical Society is to discover, memorialize and disseminate the prehistory and history of the City of Wildwood, Missouri by: (1) searching for and procuring written or photographic documentation (including but not limited to personal writings or photographs, newspaper articles, blueprints, maps, journals, cemetery records, and genealogical records), artifacts, relics, memorabilia, and/or other similar documents, items, or objects relating to the prehistory and history of Wildwood; (2) preserving, displaying, and making available to the public these documents, items and objects by placing them in a museum/library/research center and in exhibits strategically located throughout Wildwood; (3) identifying and helping to maintain and preserve historic and prehistoric homes, buildings and/or other significant structures and/or sites; (4) maintaining an active outreach and education program for Society members and the general public; and, (5) accepting donations of money, real property and/or other property as appropriate to accomplish the above.

COMMUNITY ORGANIZATIONS

Every Wildwood Day, the Wildwood Historical Society hosts a display of their extensive collection of vintage photos and artifacts, and members are available to talk about area history. Here, Dorothy Pendleton and a Wildwood Day visitor look at one of the photo displays.

Glencoe School, 1916. Top row, left to right: Elizabeth Kunze, Margaret Williams, Kathryn Leibig, teacher, Theodore Klenigusti, Everett _____, Bernard Evert, Enous Woolen. Second row: Mildred Goff, Aldoph Haud, Margaret Halley, Margie Goff, Lena McDaniel, Bessie Drenning, Annie Loeffel, Ollie Harness, Raymond Goff. Third row: Tony and Sam McDaniel, Andy Lewis, Stan Hanlon, Bizzie Roenet, Mary Bell Carbon, Annette Stossie, Emma Loeffel, Everett Harness, Ivy Lewis, Harry McDaniel. The 1911 History of St. Louis County lists District 62 Glencoe School officers as William McQuibban, clerk, and John F. Beard, director. This building burned and was replaced with a different structure.

Chapter 4
SCHOOLS

From the time of earliest settlement, area residents have placed a high priority on education. From preschools to colleges, Wildwood residents have lots of choices available and more are being built every year. In addition to the educational institutions within Wildwood borders, there are many colleges and private schools within commuting distance.

Wild Horse School students, late 1920s.

St. Louis Community College at Wildwood

St. Louis Community College at Wildwood's campus was a welcome addition to the community when it opened in the fall of 2007. It is the largest Leadership in Energy and Environmental Design™ (LEED) gold-level certified community college facility in the United States. It is the fourth campus in the STLCC system, which has a reputation for excellent, affordable transfer education and high quality workforce training.

The section of land now occupied by the St. Louis Community College campus and the YMCA were once part of a large farm owned by the Wright family. The family home was across Highway 109, where Rockwood Bank and the business center are now located. Part of the Wright farm was sold to the Bader family, who owned and operated Bader's Meat Market for many years. The market was sold and the building torn down to make way for the YMCA.

The initial building, 75,000 square feet, houses high-tech classrooms and labs, a library, an academic support center, student services, lounges, a bookstore, multipurpose room, and classrooms equipped with sophisticated presentation and web-based technologies that will allow faculty to help stimulate different learning styles and clarify difficult concepts. It also provides high-speed Internet access by cable as well as wireless connectivity within and around the campus site. Future site development is planned.

SCHOOLS

The new St. Louis Community College campus in Wildwood.

The eco-friendly, state-of-the-art Wildwood campus can serve up to two thousand students. It offers associate degree programs in business administration, general transfer studies, and teaching, as well as introductory career courses and developmental courses needed to attain degrees. Through a partnership with the University of Missouri–St. Louis, students can take courses at Wildwood that will lead to bachelor's degrees in business administration, liberal studies or elementary education. The Wildwood campus is located at 2645 Generations Drive, Wildwood, MO 63040-1168, near the intersection of Route 109 and Manchester Road. For more information about their programs, call (636)422-2000 or visit their website, www.stlcc.edu.

Wildwood Public Schools— Rockwood School District

P rior to 1949, each community in the Wildwood area had its own school. These were one-room schools in most cases, with all the grades one through eight being taught by one teacher. The schools were called Hollow, Melrose, Wild Horse, Sherman, Smith, Orrville, Orrville African American, Glencoe, and Pond. Reorganization of the schools began in October of 1949, and it took two years to complete. The small schools were closed, and students then attended the Rockwood R-6 district, with its central office at Eureka. The name "Rockwood" was adopted due to the most prominent natural resources of our area—rocks and woods.

Elementary students from the Glencoe School went to Eureka Elementary. Those from Orrville went to Chesterfield Elementary, and

| Smith School with students, early 1920s. William Andrea was the teacher.

SCHOOLS

Smith School, 1947

those from Hollow, Melrose, Wild Horse, Smith, and Pond schools attended the new Pond Elementary School, which opened in 1952 with eight classrooms for grades one through six. Seventh and eighth grade students went to Ballwin School until completion of the Crestview Junior High in 1955. That building is now called Babler Elementary School.

Integration occurred in 1964, when African American schools were closed and their students were sent to neighboring schools.

The building currently housing Crestview Middle School was originally the Lafayette Senior High School, which opened in 1960. Prior to that, all senior high school students attended Eureka High School. The new Lafayette High School was opened in 1989.

In 1993, the middle school plan was adopted and La Salle Springs and Rockwood Valley Middle schools were opened in Wildwood. In 2001, Wildwood Middle School on Old Manchester Road was opened. In addition to elementary, middle, and high schools, Rockwood has many locations for preschool and summer child care.

SCHOOLS

| Lafayette High School

| Rockwood Valley Middle School

Fairway Elementary School

Other schools in Wildwood include:

Hope Montessori Academy
16554 Clayton Road
636-458-4540
Preschool through Grade 1

Apple Hill Academy
16290 Pierside Lane
636-458-4323
applehillacademy.com
Preschool

Wildwood Christian School
Located in Heritage Presbyterian Church
4000 Alt Road
Grades 7 through 12

St. Alban Roe Catholic School
2005 Shepard Road
636-458-6084
Grades K through 8

SCHOOLS

West County Christian Academy
Located at Bethel Church
17500 Manchester Road
636-273-5922
Pre-K through 3

Elegant Child
513 Strecker Road
Phone: 636-458-4414
www.elegantchildcampus.com
Pre K and K

Elaine Rosi Academy for children
1725 Hwy 109
www.rosiacademy.com
636-405-0075
Preschool and day care for children from 6 weeks to 12 years.

Pierside Kindercare
16375 Pierside Lane
636-458-3000
Childcare/Preschool
kindercare.com

| Wildwood Middle School

SCHOOLS

Eureka High School football players, 1940s. There were few high schools in the Wildwood area in the first half of the 1900s. In 1931, the Missouri Legislature passed a law that any school district that lacked a high school had to pay to send their students to a district that did have a high school. As a result, Eureka High School's enrollment swelled with students from as far away as Kirkwood. By 1933, there were three buses picking up students all over the area. Students in the southern half of Wildwood attend Eureka High School. Pictured in this photo are, left to right in front: Clark Casey, Richard Bacon, Ervin Schaedler, unknown, Spencer Waddell, Gardner Hausman, unknown. Boys in the back row are unknown.

Eureka High School

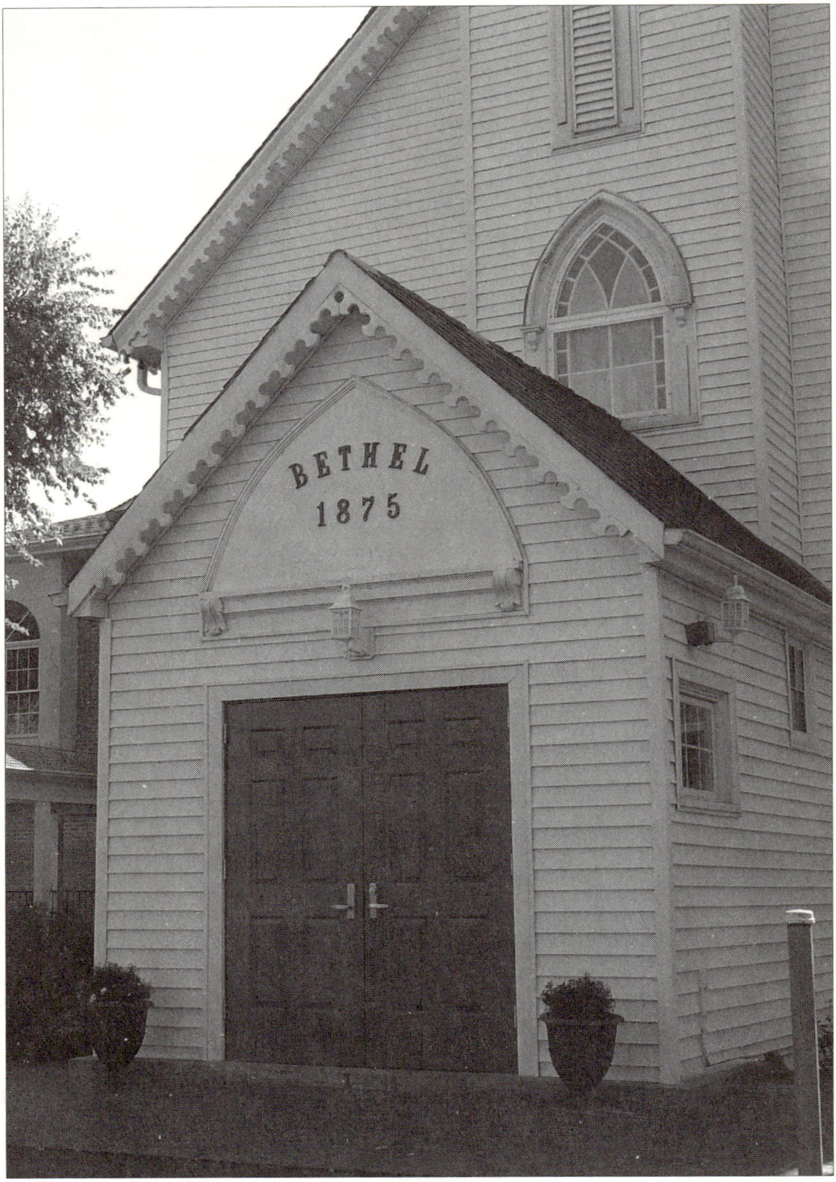
BETHEL
1875

Chapter 5
CHURCHES

The people who settled Wildwood immediately began to organize churches of many denominations. For rural residents, the church offered a community and ways to socialize; many traditions include annual chicken dinners, bazaars, box socials, May crownings, and other events. In recent decades, especially, the congregations of faith offer stability in a changing world.

Due to Wildwood's sprawling size, this listing of churches doesn't represent all of the options that residents have for a faith community. In addition to the churches within Wildwood's borders, many residents attend churches in Chesterfield, Eureka, Pacific, Ellisville, and other surrounding cities.

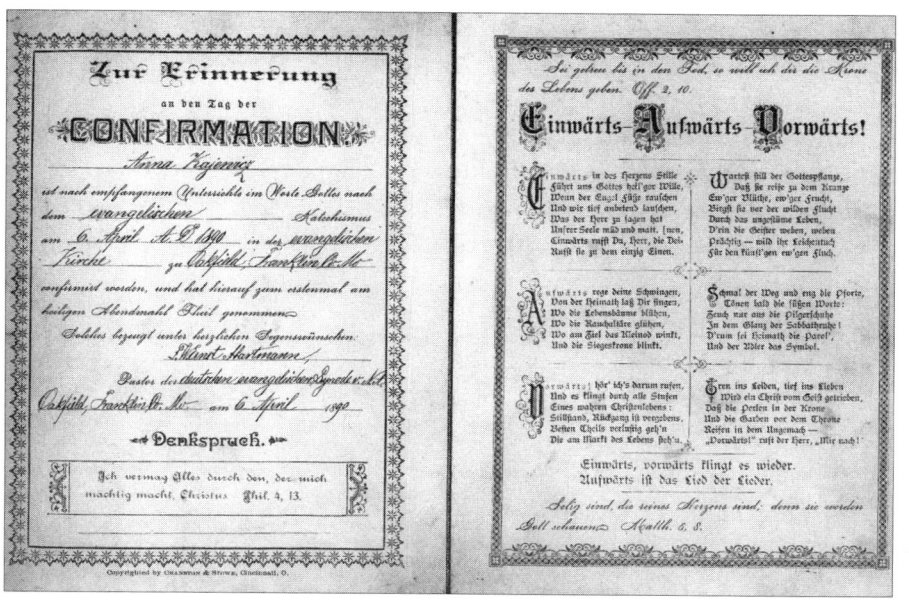

Anna Kajewicz's confirmation certificate from Oakfield Church, just over the Franklin County Line. Note that the document is in German. Anna and her family lived in the Fox Creek area.

Bethel United Methodist Church and Cemetery

Bethel Church is one of the oldest institutions in Wildwood. The Hebrew word *Bethel* means "House of God." The historic church got its beginnings in 1858, when a group of Southern Methodist preachers were holding a meeting near "Camp Hollow" in western St. Louis County.

A year later, a stone church called Rock Bethel was dedicated on Wild Horse Creek. After the Civil War, the congregation moved to a log building in Gaehle's Grove, at the junction of Wild Horse Creek and Hardt roads. In 1873, the St. Louis Marble Company donated two acres on Manchester Road, and additional land was purchased from that company for a cemetery. This beautiful cemetery remains the main burying ground in the Wildwood area for people of all faiths. The new church was dedicated in April 1875.

These historic views of Bethel Church were drawn by Wildwood artist Michael Haynes.

CHURCHES

CHURCHES

Living Word United Methodist Church. Living Word's first worship service was held in 1962 at Ellisville Elementary School. The church had 115 charter members. The next year, the congregation moved to their new church at 15977 Clayton Road in Ellisville. From 1962 to 2007, the church was known as Ellisville United Methodist Church and was renamed Living Word United Methodist Church. The church moved to 17315 Manchester Road, their new Wildwood site, on April 6, 2008.

West County Community Church is at 17770 Mueller Road.

CHURCHES

Pastor Jerry Marshall leads a service, 2008. On Sunday, April 30, 1989, Pastor Marshall and sixty-seven people gathered for the first worship of New Community Church at 16801 Manchester Road.

St. Paul Lutheran Church, a member of the Lutheran Church, Missouri Synod, is celebrating its 125th year in 2008. This country congregation began in 1883. St. Paul's adjoining burying ground reads like "Who's Who" in Wildwood. Some of the family names represented include: Von Gruben, St. Onge, Pauble, Poertner, Fick, Wardenburg, Hohmann, Essen, Kern, Gaehle, Schaeg, Krausch, Hatz, and Schott.

BIBLIOGRAPHY

Bek, William G., "The Followers of Duden," *Missouri Historical Review*, Series, 1919–1921.

Berry, Dovie, numerous letters, papers, and articles on local history topics.

Brown, Susan K., "Living History: Plantations Yield Data on Slaves," *St. Louis Post-Dispatch*, 16 October 1989.

Foster, Al, *Glencoe, From the Beginning* (St. Louis, 1983).

Daub, Chylene Jaun, *History of Ellisville, Missouri* (City of Ellisville, 1983).

J. Thomas Scharf, *History of Saint Louis City and County*, 2 Vols. (Philadelphia: Louis H. Everts & Co., 1883).

Pendleton, Dorothy, *Wildwood Schools*.

Pitzman, Julius, *Pitzman's New Atlas of the City and County of St. Louis, Missouri* (Philadelphia: B. Holcombe Company, 1878).

Schaedler, Ervin, Schaedler Family and Wildwood history topics, handwritten papers.

Shankland, W.M., *A Saga of the Coleman's of Centaur* (St. Louis, 1970).

The Past in Our Presence: Historic Buildings in St. Louis County (St. Louis County, 1996).

Thomas, William Lyman, *History of St. Louis County, Missouri*, 2 Vols. (St. Louis: S.J. Clarke Publishing Co., 1911).

Wilmot, David, *A History of Eureka, Missouri* (St. Louis County Planning Commission, 1979).

Wyatt, Steve, "Rockwood Reservation History," *Making Tracks Newsletter*, Series, 1997–1998.

Interviews with Author:

Becker, Brother Marvin, 1996.
Berry, Dovie, 1996–2000.
Boyd, Maude Poe, April–September 1996.
Connolly, Brother Kent, 1996.
Conreaux, Lorraine, 1996.
Cullinane, Sue, October–November 2008.
Frazier, Clifford, 1997.
Gaehle, Barney, 1996.
Grauer, Ethel Lynn, 1997.
Hairston, Irene, 1996–1997.
Hoehne, Glen "Cotton," 1996–2007.
Jaeger, Don, 1997.
Kelpe, Claude, 1997.
Kreienkamp, Stanley and Carmen, 1996.
Leiweke, Robert, April 1996.
McKenzie, Bebe, 1996–2008.
Musenbrock, Helen Schlemper, 1996–2008.
Pendleton, Dorothy and Rusty, 1996–2008.
Poe, Francis Hill, March 1996.
Ries, Amelia Morgan, 1997.
Schaedler, Ervin, 1996–1997.
Schlemper, Emma, April–August 1996.
Sheehan, Jack, 1996–1998.
Ward, Paul, 1997.
Wilson, Earl, 1996–1998.